Saving
Heroes

Dr Burke masterfully sheds light on a dark and often taboo subject. PTSD is a real and present danger for many of our heroes. Get this book for a friend.... get this book for a loved one..... get this book for yourself! It is a difference maker. Let his journey, struggle, and faith inspire you and or someone you care about.

Joe Dixon
Fire Chief, Goldsboro Fire Department, NC

In *Saving Heroes*, Dr. Burke uncovers the foundation for winning the hidden war with traumatic stress and introduces the concept of spiritual combat training. His innovative approach for addressing the complex issues of traumatic stress will prove valuable to chaplains, military leaders, first responders, religious leaders, and medical professionals.

Semper Fi,
Faron Golden
Retired First Sergeant of Marines
CEO, Heptagon Information Technology

Saving Heroes is a one-stop shop for America's best practices in suicide prevention. Matthew's success in healing our military and first responder personnel and their families is a testament to his findings. Great mixture of religion and science, truly covering holistic health and wellness...

John W. Phillips
Civilian Aide to the Secretary of the Army – Georgia (North)
Co-Founder & Vice President, VETLANTA
Founder & Executive Director, Boots to Loafers, LLC.
Lieutenant Colonel, USA {R}

Dr. Matthew Burke has shared his powerful and touching journey in his book *Saving Heroes*. Through his transparency in documenting his own struggles and triumphs through the lens of his experience with PTSD, I have no question he will offer others in similar circumstances faith, guidance, and a calm in the storm.

Tina Jaeckle, Ph.D., LCSW
Crisis and Trauma Clinician, Consultant, and Instructor
Law Enforcement and First Responders

Dr. Burke's personal experience and research have caught the essence of the men and women facing PTSD. Through his own experience, he has gained an insight into this problem that faces so many. As Sheriff, I have had men and women facing PTSD, many of who have had to leave the profession that they loved. Most recently a deputy sheriff was involved in a movie theater shooting. Due to this experience, he developed PTSD and had to give up the job he had devoted his life to. No matter what profession you are in, PTSD is very real and can cause uncontrollable stress which can change a life.

Sheriff William O. "Bill" Farmer Jr.
Sumter County, Florida

Saving Heroes

A Warrior's Journey through Rehabilitation

Matthew R. Burke, Ph.D.

WestBow
PRESS®
A DIVISION OF THOMAS NELSON
& ZONDERVAN

This book is a work of non-fiction. Unless otherwise noted, the author and the publisher make no explicit guarantees as to the accuracy of the information contained in this book and in some cases, names of people and places have been altered to protect their privacy.

WestBow Press books may be ordered through booksellers or by contacting:

WestBow Press
A Division of Thomas Nelson & Zondervan
1663 Liberty Drive
Bloomington, IN 47403
www.westbowpress.com
844-714-3454

Scripture taken from the King James Version of the Bible.

ISBN: 978-1-6642-0979-4 (sc)
ISBN: 978-1-6642-0980-0 (hc)
ISBN: 978-1-6642-0978-7 (e)

Library of Congress Control Number: 2020920724

Print information available on the last page.

WestBow Press rev. date: 05/10/2021

This book is dedicated to the brave men and women in uniform who have valiantly served in the military, law enforcement, and fire-rescue. Furthermore, to your families who endure the hardship of your sacrifices. May God bless, keep, and comfort you. Saving Heroes is a product of my second chance. May God receive the glory!

To my wife, the world's greatest Hidden Hero, thank you for believing in me. To my daughters, Jasmine and Adina, thank you for the amazing adventure of fatherhood. To my parents, your leadership and guidance birthed my purpose-driven life. To my brothers and sister, this book is a product of our crazy years together.

CONTENTS

INTRODUCTION

Saving Heroes provides a glimpse into a combat veteran's quest to overcome post-traumatic stress disorder (PTSD) and suicidal ideations. Redirecting attention from the war on terror in Afghanistan to the battlefield within provided the strength and knowledge to help hometown heroes and their families. From spiritual combat training to rescuing emotional POWs, this journey will lead you through the darkness into the light of hope and freedom.

Compressing fifteen years of research and development, firsthand experiences, and biblical wisdom, created a solution to the world's mental health crisis. It is a manual for suicide prevention and a formula to treat PTS (removing the stigma of "disorder"). *Saving Heroes* is devoted to the men and women entrenched in spiritual warfare and is a proven battle plan. It does not replace the exceptional work of the Church, medical practitioners, therapeutic programs, or the like. Instead, *Saving Heroes* complements, unites, and consolidates their efforts; extracts best practices; and offers a one-stop shop for those suffering internal turmoil. The back-to-basics approach untangles common knowledge for the uncommon warrior. "Many persons have the wrong idea of what constitutes true happiness. It is not obtained through self-gratification, but through fidelity to a worthy purpose" (Helen Keller).

Human thought is often governed by culture. Visionaries explore ideas beyond social norms but face rebuke for untimely innovation. Some knowledge inside this book is borrowed to reinforce my discovery. Sources are cited as accurately as possible, but some information may be unknowingly replicated. It is not my intention to own any one thought but to capitalize on our spiritual connection for a common interest. I do not seek glory but opportunity. Allow me to share my testimony, unveil a plan to rescue spiritual POWs, and bridge the gap between the Church and our warriors.

This book is designed to enhance ministries, government entities, and nonprofit efforts. It is written with a heart of grace, mercy, and love. If you read this book through the lens of love, then you will discover a world-changing solution. Those who seek flaws will find them because I too am human. Though I grew up in church, worldly temptations gently pulled me away. Parental pressure accelerated my departure, but marriage and a child brought me back. Returning to Christ was easier than running away. There were stipulations to my damnation but no conditions for my return. Understanding the law convicted me into repentance, and forgiveness graced me with salvation. Many church leaders, however, were unhelpful in my rehabilitation.

My fourth military deployment landed me in Afghanistan. I was a squadron leader supervising nearly fifty Airmen and seven combat aircraft. I was injured during a major attack but didn't seek immediate help. My injuries progressively got worse and eventually led to PTSD and physical disability. My actions were not of valor but of duty to my faith, family, and country. Landing in a wheelchair was humiliating, and my lack of progress led to a medical retirement. I vowed to continue serving, and though I suffered homelessness after out-processing, I founded a not-for-profit organization to stay my purpose. What I didn't realize is that my purpose would lead to a cure that works for me and may work for others.

Within this book are simple answers to complicated problems. To accept it is to acknowledge the mighty power of God. To reject it is to deny the truth that everyone, even you, has a purpose for being where you are in this moment. I hope and pray that the divine inspiration that led to this book motivates you to take a deeper look. I once believed that a cure for PTSD did not exist. My past skepticism helps me empathize with so many others who still refuse to believe they can overcome it. We claim and believe that it's something we have to learn to cope with, but I—we—were wrong. Let the journey begin.

1

A Warrior's Revival

It was an average evening on the farm in Webster, Florida, as my wife and I prepared for bed. My youngest daughter slept in the room nearby. As we laid there, I heard what I thought was a jet aircraft. The sound grew louder and more abrupt, like it was nose diving towards earth. As I peered out the east window, I quickly located the source high in the sky. It appeared to be a fighter jet at full speed on a crash course. It sped up, and the noise screamed louder until it struck the ground far off in the distance. The earth shook, and a shockwave hit me before I saw the mushroom cloud. Cracking, popping, and a tremendous roar echoed in the distance. I could see a wall of rolling smoke, grayish black with fire inside, speeding toward me. My heart raced, and my mind searched for what to do. We had no bunker in which to seek shelter and no time to run. I was unprepared for this moment. I grabbed my wife from the bed and drug her off the opposite side. As she frantically questioned me, I laid on top in a desperate attempt to shelter her from the incoming, all-consuming furnace. Instead of explaining, I began to pray. I prayed for my soul, for the salvation of my family and friends, and for another chance. I prayed to survive this, knowing that nothing else would matter but sharing Him with them. And then it happened—my second chance.

I woke early on June 7, 2020, after suffering yet another nightmare stimulated by PTS. Tropical Storm Cristobal stewed in the Gulf of Mexico, riots and protests had spread across the United States, and the COVID-19 pandemic was slowly losing its grip on our quarantined country. Crime and domestic terrorism haunt communities, families are falling apart, and segregation has disguised itself as theology.

The steady rain beat upon the metal roof of my farmhouse in Newberry. My pup, Avery, was by my side as I lay in our guest room. My mind raced to find meaning in the nightmare, a reminder, possibly, that I'm already living in my second chance. I woke earlier that morning from another series of nightmares that weren't as riveting, snuck out of my bedroom, and stealthily checked all the doors and windows. Secured.

This nightly routine is a regimen of sleeplessness that I suffer because of my experience in Afghanistan. The unimaginable horrors of war haunt my subconscious. But I found a working cure—a formula that I once didn't think existed. The bread-crumb trail leading me to this cure was a hard reset on my purpose in life.

I once thought that serving my country at the highest levels was my destiny, and I wanted that. But on September 10, 2011, at Bagram Airfield in Afghanistan, that changed. My thirteen years in the Air Force came to an end when it was decided that my rehabilitation was failing to progress. The medical community, psychologist, and military threw everything they had at helping me get better, while the Church sat idly by. I refused to accept the possibility that I'd ever get past this. The physical pain resonating from my injuries, my disabilities, and emotional limitations changed me from whom I once was.

As a believer in a higher power—in God, in Jesus Christ—I found refuge in the thought that there was purpose in my suffering, that God had saved me for a reason. My life for the previous seven years had been devoted to this second chance and to bridging the gap between warriors and the Church. But as I laid there by my pup, praying for support, I was reminded that I'm lucky to be alive.

The wall of destruction that combined the power of a tornado, volcano, and earthquake shook me to my senses. Praying for God to deliver more funds, more volunteers, and more opportunities was not the right prayer. Yes, those things matter, but the fact is that saving just one is sufficient.

Spiritual Apocalypse

A plague is destroying humanity, but an antidote exists to help us survive it. Love, grace, and mercy triumph over hate, greed, lust, and self-destruction. Freedom from self-imprisonment is a personal choice. This is a call to action, an emotional stimulator with cognitive enlightenment. If reading through the content of this book sparks nothing, then I have failed you. Anger, doubt, indifference, and drawbacks may arise, but I urge you to continue forward because those are the barriers you must overcome before discovering your cure.

Pushing forward allows you to find the peace that passes all understanding, the unspeakable joy, the purest form of unconditional love. You'll discover forgiveness, liberating repentance, and salvation. The world is better with you in it, so don't quit.

Countless studies around the world reveal the complex phenomenon of suicide. Some research points to a chemical imbalance while others to physical or emotional pain. Nearly everyone has dealt with self-infliction. For many, that's suicidal thoughts. No matter how you say it, "die by suicide" or "commit suicide," the result is the same. In a time of political correctness, death by suicide continues to happen. So obviously what we call it has no bearing.

As a survivor of this spiritual war, I'm entitled to speak bold truth. My intentions are pure and driven by love. It's easy to object, criticize, and nullify my findings, and that's okay. My mission is to fulfill this journey of enlightenment by sharing my testimony. It's not religiously or politically driven. It's biblical, empirical, academic, and unbiased. I have one agenda: to save you from yourself.

It takes courage to speak on this matter, as we often fear what others think. This book draws intelligence from various sources and pulls no punches. It may sting those who have lost someone to suicide, upset practitioners and religious leaders, and draw fire from skeptics. I have and will face persecution, but I'm ready for it.

The well of life must be found individually. Accept the terms of life, that each of us are personally accountable for ourselves. Many people who struggle with suicidal ideations can overcome them through training.

Education, spirituality, combat training, and perseverance were weapons I choose to conquer my enemy. This book can be your key to victory. It combines science and religion. The solution can be confusing, so let me simplify it. The delivery mechanism is grace, mercy, and tough love. It is a collection of knowledge pieced together as a manual for warriors struggling with moral wounds. Practitioners and religious leaders can glean insight as well.

We strive to gain full understanding. Our aspirations lead us to explore new pathways, but they often take us down roads that are well traveled. God decrees all conceivable knowledge, and most of it is in the Bible. Countless hours and billions of dollars are spent on recreating the wheel. Thousands of studies on one sample may produce different results, but facts and truth are never changing. One can manipulate them to fit their agenda or pleasure, but it doesn't amount to the truth. It is right, or it is wrong; there are boys, and there are girls; we either live free, or we die captive.

Mental health is a direct reflection of spiritual wellness. If we view spirituality in a tangible sense, then we can better understand and treat traumatic stress. I deduce is that a virus has infected our psychology.

This spiritual virus corrupts the mind, body, and soul. It begins like other viruses or infections and then spreads like an Oklahoma wildfire on a dry, windy day. However, a spiritual virus is unlike any disease known to humankind and requires an intangible treatment plan. It often starts in childhood, lingers for years, and rears its head during traumatic experiences.

Spiritual infections are proponents of a virus that can be controlled and even cured with an invasive lifestyle change. Examples of these infections are PTSD, secondary traumatic stress (STS), vicarious trauma, anxiety, depression, and many other mental health issues. We must implement control measures that are more proactive than reactive. Curing spiritual infections can stop self-destructive behaviors. You have the keys to unlock the prison door that keeps you captive. Escaping is not easy, and you alone are responsible for your freedom. People along the way will provide tools, resources, and cheer you on. But those you leave behind in their self-imprisonment will attempt to diminish your efforts. Sharing your strategic plan with them is essential, but do not return to this place until you're ready to join our ranks as special forces in spiritual warfare. If you are currently suffering from ideas of self-destruction, then take the following steps:

1. Call 9-1-1 and let the dispatcher know that you feel like hurting yourself. The dispatcher will want to remain on the phone with you until rescue arrives. If it's safe, go outside with only this book and your phone and wait for their arrival. The sole purpose of 9-1-1 is to save lives. There is little difference between an armed robber holding you hostage and your current state of mind. Take this step immediately. The enemy surrounds you, and it's time to call in reinforcements. Let others help you. The stigma of being suicidal is only harmful if it becomes you.

    a. If you don't have 9-1-1 services because you're deployed, then connect with your chaplain or first sergeant; they are trained to help. If it's only you and your spotter, then seek their confidence because they have your six. Becoming vulnerable will take more courage than holding your position against an onslaught of enemy fire. Let God work through your battle buddy.

    b. If you are in prison, then confide in the visiting minister or a guard. Guards train to keep you safe in addition to realigning your social behavior. Don't fit into cultural norms? No sweat— neither do many of us. God created you with a unique talent. It is your choice to use that talent for good or evil.

    c. If you are in another country that has a unique emergency response system, then call them. If you don't have one, then reach out to an elder in your family, tribe, or community and explain to them your feelings. Believe it or not, we're all under the same authority and in the same spiritual war. Different cultures have unique ways of combating these attacks. We are interested in hearing from you on methods used in your area.

2. Turn to chapter 3 and get right to it. All other chapters in this book enhance chapter 3 through traditional means: educating, improving, and providing data for your cure. You can go back and read the remaining information later when you're safe (hence the need to take the book with you).

3. The only way you're letting anyone down is by tapping out don't fight this battle alone. Every warrior has a team; there are no exceptions. You are a highly sought-after asset. Organizations across the world are recruiting people like you, so find a unit to join. Plug in!

If your suffering is intermittent, then continue reading this book chronologically. Skipping ahead cheats you from the full effect. Fight the urge for instant gratification and invest your time in absorbing the material diligently. Leaders, it will help you not only save a warrior but countless others who suffer from similar attacks. Millions across America consider suicide on a daily occurrence. Everyone's battle is unique, but the results are the same. Learning to live sacrificially is the most challenging yet rewarding lifestyle. Most of us want our lives to mean something, but what about our deaths?

Dying is inevitable. No one cheats it unless, of course, you believe in spiritual eternity (John 3:16; John 17:3; Matthew 25:46). Romans 6:23 notes that "the wages of sin is death, but the gift of God (His Son) is eternal life." Your death can occur at any moment. You can either give it sacrificially for the greater good as a martyr or waste it for nothing as a statistic. What do you profit if you gain the world but lose your soul (Matthew 16:24–26)? The latter occurs when you choose to check out before the game's over. As a martyr, you give your life for a purpose.

Matthew 22:14 states, "Many are called, but few are chosen." Some don't know how to listen for the call, while others are too busy to hear the ring. Constant chatter (busyness) creates white noise in our spirits that hinders our ability to hear God. Some of us lack the courage to answer; others force our will into the equation. Waiting on the call is just as important as answering it when it happens. The complexities of society can be overwhelming. Don't mute your ringer.

In the military, we use the phrase "fit to fight." We exercise daily to keep our minds and bodies prepared for any given situation because we provide America's security twenty-four-seven. This model is missing a key element, though—spiritual readiness. Spiritual readiness defends us against infections. The hidden battle of moral wounds is wildly complex yet checkbox simple. When you've obtained the most authentic essence of fit to fight, you become an elite, efficient, resilient warrior.

I was locked into a military contract when I received my calling in 2005. This obligation didn't stop me, however. My purpose was clear, but the how, when, and why were not. I marched forward to begin prepping myself for the road ahead. I invested over fifteen years in researching, developing, practicing, exploring, and obtaining the highest level of education, all while succumbing to a traumatic event that nearly knocked me out of play.

Like many souls before me, deciphering God's call on my life began long before He rang my bell. I attribute my injury during an attack in Afghanistan to God's merciful plan for my life. Though it was challenging to obtain this perspective, it's what separates pessimism from optimism in my life.

You cannot measure or weigh a soul. Big organizations invest little stock in spiritual welfare. The uncalculatable data often deters investors, as most people want to see how their funds are impacting the mission. Having something tangible, weighable, and measurable is more understandable. It is an unpleasant necessity that ensures mission effectiveness. By investing your time and treasure into this book, you will discover a working cure for mental health issues.

We're in the age of charitable endeavors, each program doing amazing work towards the solution. Although each organization has answers, it's the hierarchy epidemic that hinders our ability to unite. Academia has created a generation of leaders, social change agents, and philosophers. But farmers and tradespeople have been shunned, as well as obedient followers.

We are top-heavy in leadership. Everyone wants to be the captain of the ship. I was guilty of this until my mother realized my perspective. She said, "Matthew, not everyone can be the captain of the ship. We require people to swab the deck, handle the sails, and watch for hazards." It was at that moment that I genuinely understood how vital followership is in the big picture.

The US military is world dominant because it has mastered the chain of command. While each branch has its unique specialties, the ability for them to function synergistically has created a global superpower. Imagine if this were true of nonprofits and churches. Take a moment to visualize the global impact of unity. Now, accept the reality that our division within charitable endeavors and churches have created a weakness. I believe this goes much deeper than academia or technology. It is our desire to be remembered, to leave our mark, and to have a legacy. It's the pursuit of being relevant that drives our purpose, which has led to a division.

Some claim that many reasons exist for one to commit suicide: PTS, chronic pain, financial difficulties, mental health—and the list goes on. My goal is to condense this down to one cause and provide ten life elements for a cure. If you have ever thought of hurting yourself or someone else, know someone that fits this bill, or want to help those who are struggling, then please unite with us.

Serving is easy; it's navigating the skeptics, critics, and plagiarizers that often destroys a charitable soul. Add to that the competitive nature of nonprofiteering, and you'd surely find many good doers closing up shop. Statistics show that businesses don't last beyond three years. This statistic is a driving force behind the legacy of a warrior's ethos.

Let's not water down the term *warrior*. Unless you've been a combatant, you're not a warrior. You can be a hero; that's a different category. Warriors fight! They enforce the law, defend our country, and run toward danger (fighting fires and saving lives). Heroes are symbols of hope in dire times. A warrior can be a hero at any given moment, but a hero cannot be a warrior unless they are physically involved in a fight. A Christian warrior is not someone who has a war room for prayer. While praying is the most powerful thing you can do, a Christian warrior is someone who keeps the faith during the battle. Spiritual warfare is a whole different category.

Battlefields can be destructive or constructive. Some of the greatest lessons we learned originate on the battlefield. New technology and tactics, even cultural shifts. Imagine if the South would have won the US Civil War. Now visualize what WWII would have looked like without the United States' intervention. We could all be speaking German or Japanese. What if we had lost the Revolutionary War; would we be a free nation? Battles shape us as people. Sometimes this molding process is too much for individuals to handle. It is, after all, a pivot point in our lives.

Every warrior is affected differently—some physically, others psychologically, but all spiritually. Spiritual warfare is the most challenging battle we face. While books like the Bible provide tactical training for spirituality, it is often incomprehensible because it is intangible. We train to calculate and execute decisions for success, but who defines what success looks like?

Cultures manipulate the definition of *success*. Winning your spiritual war is like the never-ending battle on terrorism, and we must approach it as such. We must redefine what success looks like and realize that the hidden enemy will attack us at our weakest points and at times when we least expect it. We will take losses on the battlefield, but we can still win this war if we're willing to be a kamikaze for our belief.

It Takes One to Know One

Growing up in poverty on a small farm in Webster, Florida, my father, an Army Green Beret, left when I was eleven years old. I learned to live off the land: farming, hunting, fishing, and foraging for sustenance. My mother recounts, "Matthew would bring home some peculiar animals, clean them, then prepare a meal for everyone. He took pride in providing for us." Fortunately, she worked diligently to escape poverty, but restoring a broken home wasn't as easy.

Several men came and went, trying to fill the father-figure void. Two of them were abusive and didn't last long. The last stepfather who remained wasn't perfect, but he was what our family needed. In the process of rebuilding, two more sons were born, for a total of five children. The oldest is a Purple Heart recipient from Operation Iraqi Freedom; my sister was a law enforcement officer before being seriously injured in an ATV accident; and the two younger brothers are talented musicians and artists. There's much more to my siblings though.

Rather than being a high school scholar, I was a misfit and a C-average student. I grew up in church and learned right from wrong by testing the line. As a tactile learner, I leaned on adults and my older brother for mentorship. He didn't recognize the importance of his role, and most of the adults in my life either discounted me or abused their authority. One male role model who didn't falter was my baseball coach, Mike Foote, Sr. He stands out as being a man of courage because he believed in me and treated me as a valuable member of the community. Several other men, like my uncles and my grandfather (Korean War veteran), all played a part in developing my outlook on life and, ultimately, this book. It is my childhood that shaped my manhood, but only I can dictate my perception.

After mixing it up with the wrong group of friends and being led down a dead-end road, I vowed to make a change. Seeking a cleansing from the culture I had engulfed myself in, I moved to Kentucky with my father. There, I began the healing process of forgiveness and recompense. I returned to college with academia on my mind but soon found the beauty of women at college a distraction.

One student, an Asian girl, stood out from the rest. Her exotic beauty was more than I could handle from afar; I needed to know her intimately. I began designing a game plan to make my move, but on game day, I smelled like a skunk (literally). I could not deviate as everything was already in motion, and she bore my horrifying smell like a champ. I knew she was the one.

Although I was at my lowest point in life, living in a five-foot-by-ten-foot loft above barn animals, I kept hope alive. As our relationship grew, she became curious about my living conditions and requested a visit. Reluctantly, I agreed, thinking this would be the end. Her reaction and divergent behavior unexpectedly ignited a passionate moment, which led to a surprising inception.

When the news arrived that she was pregnant, our previous pro-life conversations resulted in the most challenging decision of my life. Decisions are easy when they align with your plans, but a person's character reveals itself in unplanned circumstances. After lengthy conversations and much prayer, we sided with our consciences and chose to marry. Deciding to commit was the single best decision of my life, the pivot point that turned everything around. It was a divine intervention that led to my leaving thug life for real life.

We married in the fall of 1999, and I managed to scrounge up five hundred dollars for the entire wedding. Even though few friends and family showed, we had a fantastic ceremony. I dropped college and became an emergency medical technician and firefighter. We moved into a trailer down Rifle Range Road and began our lives as one. I knew we didn't have much support in Kentucky for the birth of our child, and I remembered how supportive our family in Florida is for one another. After convincing my wife to leave her friends and family for mine, we packed up and headed south. My expectation that my entire family would show up at the hospital resulted in catastrophic disappointment. It wasn't until my rebirth in combat over ten years later that I eventually found the strength to forgive them.

While struggling to make ends meet and bouncing from job to job to support my family, the idea of joining the military arose. With her agreement, I enlisted in the Air Force in 2000 and was shipped to the great state of Texas. Our daughter was only seven months old at the time. It was a tough decision to leave my young family, and the sacrifices were overwhelming. Although I yearned to reunite with them, my duty as a provider took priority. Though heartbreaking, this time away taught me how to compartmentalize and remain mission focused, which kept me alive during countless temporary-duty assignments and four combat deployments.

My first deployment and extended time away from my wife led to an overwhelming desire to make more babies. As I walked off the aircraft with a hundred other members of my unit, I quickly located my family in the crowd. My daughter was a little timid, but that could wait; my testosterone raged for my wife and our next child was conceived.

My wife became extremely ill with our newest addition, but my supervisors didn't sympathize. They kept me on duty while she was hospitalized and forced me to deploy. I transferred my wife to a Florida hospital and my child to the care of my mom. Using a wheelchair, I slowly pushed them through the airport. Fortunately, security allowed me to escort them to the gate. I rushed back to my vehicle before breaking down. I was nearly there when grief overtook me. Bursting out in tears and struggling to breathe, I fumbled around with the car keys until I unlocked the door and collapsed inside. I was shattered but bound by oath to stay the course.

What felt like hours could have been minutes. I lost all sense of time and found myself back home inside an empty house. I heard my daughter's voice echoing through the halls: "Daddy, Daddy, can we play?" Turning to alcohol temporarily numbed my pain.

After my second daughter was born, I was eager to find stability at home. I began applying for special-duty assignments that didn't involve deployments and was selected to become a recruiter. We moved from

Abilene, Texas, to Richmond, Kentucky and began my new assignment. In addition to recruiting enlisted and commissioned personnel, I used this time to research my hypothesis that military training can reshape a person's character.

After nearly five years, I was eager to get back into the fight and had conclusive evidence that disproved my theory. We accepted an assignment to Tucson, Arizona, and I received deployment orders within six months. Returning home was like the other times, with the exception that I now had two daughters bidding for my time. I loved it but was overwhelmed and needed an adjustment period. Within a year, I was back on a deployment, but this time I was sent into the heart of the war.

My two buddies and I arrived Afghanistan in a C-17 performing a combat landing. We didn't have a catered adjustment period like other deployments. It was, "Here's your rifle and ammo, a map, and attack protocols. Good luck." This wasn't our first rodeo so operating with limited instructions was no problem. Our unit filled in the blanks. Each of us was there on multidimensional levels. We were acting first sergeants, shift leaders, and technicians. Our main goal was keeping everyone safe and motivated. In doing so, my life changed forever.

On September 10, 2011, insurgents launched a large-scale attack on our base. Mortars, RPGs, and small arms rained down on us early in the evening. Our officer-in-charge had ordered everyone to report in if the assault occurred, and everyone did except one technician. I volunteered to find our missing man with one battle buddy. As we left our shelter, we hustled into the darkness, navigating by memory and dim camp lights. We could hear security forces in a gunfight on the perimeter wall. The wailing base alarms (alerting us to an attack) continued to blare. As we rushed through a series of cement bunkers, several mortars exploded nearby, and the apex of my helmet struck a cement lip hanging down from the bunker ceiling. I tasted blood, saw stars, and found myself down on one knee. I did a quick self-aid check; had my wingman confirm; then slowly rose, stumbled forward, and pushed on.

We found our missing man hunkered down in his tent. After getting him geared up, we returned to our unit. The reality and possibility of death occurring at any given time, with a slight shift in the wind, resonated deep within my soul. I wondered, *could this be my end, or am I destined for more?*

My desire to stay in the fight led to a significant decline in my health. I was ordered to report to the clinic for evaluation and received prescriptions to hold me over. My physical injury began to develop into something psychological. The horror of war was all around me. Daily attacks on our base, a mass casualty incident, and medical evacuations of wounded soldiers compiled. I'm fortunate not to have experienced what others went through outside the wire, but my injuries proved difficult.

Two years of rehabilitation with little progress left me feeling imprisoned. The time came for me to medically retire from the military. My plans to be a command chief within the next few years slipped through my hands. Though I struggled to accept this change, I recognized the liability I had become to the mission. My physical regression continued until I eventually ended up in a wheelchair. It was at this point that the Air Force Wounded Warrior Program accepted me into their ranks and introduced me to the world of adaptive sports. I began training with them as I shifted from military into civilian life, but homelessness had me focused on other priorities.

To find purpose, I returned to my original calling. Not only did developing a nonprofit give me meaning, but it gave reason for my suffering. Working on a doctorate degree, family adjustments, and escaping homelessness wasn't enough, I needed more. It was at this point that we began looking for a church home.

The process of medical retirement is intrusive. I was evaluated head to toe, inside and out. Several more years of rehabilitation for both physical injuries and PTSD failed because of the system. My family suffered the brunt of this chaos. Relieving them from this destructive monster would be the last battle I could win.

A last-ditch effort to take it to God through a local church failed because they were ill equipped to work with warriors. My decision to end the suffering and harm I was causing to my family was interrupted by God. A revival took place when I went on a hunt with my friend Eddy Corona in Arizona, an adventure that filled my spiritual tank.

With a rekindled spirit, I committed myself to God as a kamikaze for Christ. Dead to myself, I decided to return to war, but this was no ordinary war. It would be the fight of my life, sacrificing myself so that others may live. My mission would continue but with a team of people having similar experiences. It was time for God to assemble a militia for spiritual combat.

Starting at the ground level, I sought out the person who was hurt the most by our circumstances—my oldest daughter. Jasmine Burke stepped up in a significant way to hold our family together in the three years of my absence. She learned to become masterful with her emotions and endured sacrifices that only military children know. She went without so that other children could enjoy holidays free from distress or fear. Jasmine's leadership and maturity didn't allow her to have many friends. Growing up in church, she often reminded me about things I had taught her.

Unfortunately, our close relationship led to a shared emotion. Jasmine began to replicate my PTS, which led to the discovery of vicarious trauma. She knew the government and church had failed us by witnessing my continual digression and lack of support for the family dynamic. Jasmine put her ambitions aside to aid in my rehabilitation. In so doing, she assisted me in developing a program that fills the gap we experienced. Building a bridge for warriors to find healing through faith and family created a movement that has now reached millions of lives all around the world. This global reach is only possible through like-minded stakeholders who unite to save heroes. My story is a testimony shared by many warriors all around the world.

Building the Team

An essential element of personal success is surrounding yourself with individuals who share similar beliefs. Finding these cohorts may prove challenging, as we're all on our journey. It is paramount to hold high expectations but ensure they are achievable, measurable, and realistic. Friends and associates come and go. I was once told that people come into our lives for a reason, season, or lifetime. Grasping this reality has allowed me to stay operational through abandonment. You must maintain an unconquerable spirit to push forward, but don't go at it alone.

The first step toward building a team is recognizing individual limitations. The greatest athletes, most impactful politicians, and even Jesus used a team. There is no anomaly, no independence, no exemptions from this requirement. It is how God functions, how our country achieves greatness, and how we as individuals become legendary. Take heed, though; your team won't always measure up.

Transferring from military service back into civilian life was shocking. The shenanigans and ungodly behavior that exist in every element of society repulsed me. My transition was overwhelming because I placed unrealistic expectations on civilians and on fellow Christians. The discipline, loyalty, and chain of command I had grown fond of in the military were now absent. "Adapt and overcome" is a phrase I learned while serving but applying it to this transition proved most challenging. A mental health counselor advised me to lower my standards, but I refused to believe that I was alone. Instead, I created categories to safeguard against disappointment. These categories are layers in my circle of friends.

The first and innermost circle is God. Your intimate and hidden secrets are here. This is your conscience and morality. This circle should be impenetrable to darkness. Hope originates here. The next layer is for up to three people—lifelong friends who you can count on in any given situation. It should be a small, well-protected circle. The next layer is for ten to twelve friends. Akin to the twelve disciples, these are friends and family members who are part of your team. They believe in you, support your purpose, and provide tough feedback. This is a moderate transition zone. Many will come and go. The next layer is for superficial friends, or people who will be there for you when it's convenient for them. This area is a high transition zone and is influenced by your success. This circle is where fields are plowed and seeds are sown. The outer sphere is most affected when your life is shaken.

This illustration depicts how the core of your circle is centered on you and God. Relationships with God and biblical guidance shape the inner circle. This influences the middle ring, and the middle ring mentors those in the outer loop.

Imagine this circle on a massage chair. When God shakes things up, the outer sphere gets the brunt of it while the innermost circle never moves. God is with you. He has never left or forsaken you. He created you, and a part of Him is inside of you. God uses the third element of Himself, the Holy Spirit, to rotate people throughout your life. As the book of Ecclesiastes points out in chapter 3, verses 1–22, "There is a season for everything." Understanding that God moves people in and out of your life will help you cope when team members quit on you.

Loneliness is defeated by this knowledge. Those who transition throughout different spheres of my life are divinely appointed to do so. Although righteous discernment is your duty, you must not close off your circle (Proverbs 18:24).

At first, establishing a team for my health and wellness came at a cost. Lacking an understanding of these circles created chaos. I sought refuge and friendships at church but found myself in the outer ring of most Christians. My circle and purpose needed to coexist because I'm nothing without a mission.

After several years of trying inside the church walls, I decided to breach religious order and farmer wisdom. Being compelled by divine influence, I began planting seeds in the weeds. In so doing, I found freedom, friends, and a team of like-minded cohorts.

The important lesson learned is that my expectation for Christians to be neighborly is interpreted differently among the Christian community. Being considerate of other people means sacrificing personal comforts and gains so that others may prosper. An inner-circle friend who has remained with me from the beginning of my transition is Joey Wheaton. He remains there because he's selfless, courteous, and real. No matter how many burdens I cast upon him, Joey remains steadfast. Our friendship works because there's reciprocation.

Isolating expectations for each circle allows growth and healing. Search for individuals with a moral compass that aligns with biblical standards and who offer their time and talents to aid your growth. Surrounding yourself with like-minded people is vital in the healing process. However, it is critical to ensure that these people will not fuel your self-destruction. Find someone who has walked in your shoes, escaped your prison, fought your demons, and is where you want to be in life. Be wary of people who speak ill of others, as they'll do the same to you. Set personal expectations high, seek the light, and enjoy the journey.

Family is the reason I fought for this country and why I continue to fight my war for life. Devoting myself to family ensures that the most important people remain in my inner circle. Although their callings may not be the same as mine, they play a vital part in my victories. At first, my oldest daughter and I built and sailed the ship of social change. My wife volunteered countless hours in support of me, and my youngest daughter used her vocal talents. A church friend climbed aboard to assist in the initial development, but raising her own family took priority. My motto is "Et Familia Fidem," which became a general rule for volunteers who joined our team. You should never sacrifice faith or family to serve others.

The testimony of my resurrection flows abundantly. I share the good news and solution with haste because countless military, law enforcement, and fire-rescue personnel are dying daily by their own hand. Those who are ready to escape spiritual imprisonment keeps me on mission. One of our first operators was a little lady by the name of Linda Stanton. She filled my ears with promises like many well-wishers before her, but my skepticism held firm. It wasn't until she delivered on her promise that I recognized the fruit of her spirit. This lady was on fire for God, but I was confused by her lack of communion at a church.

Here was a lady who climbed aboard a faith-based ministry in full commitment but didn't attend traditional church services. It took some time to realize that she found spiritual nourishment through serving. Her stance on ministry aligned perfectly with our philosophy of evangelizing through action, adventure, and the great outdoors. Linda's ferocity in marketing gained her a director's position on our board and the nickname Linda "Buckshot" Stanton. She won the Pete Sabo Award three consecutive years for outstanding volunteerism and now has an award named after her. Although a decline in her health has her benched, she continues to serve in a different capacity.

Linda's story is like so many others' but with unique identifiers that set her apart. Like you, it all began when she was a child. The adolescent developmental process and childhood foundations embed characteristics that mold our adult lives. In 1855, Frederick Douglass noted, "It's easier to build a strong child than to fix a broken man" (Brainy Quotes, 2019). Constructing a team for your purpose is a step in the right direction. It's crucial—before you make a mess of things—to find your *why*. Your why will define your how, who, where, when, and what. *Why* is the ground on which you build your home. Is your house built on rock or sand (Matthew 7:24–27)?

Rock or Sand

The Bible provides countless metaphors involving sailors, carpenters, philosophers, engineers, farmers, hunters, fishermen, and so on. It is exclusively inclusive. The parables Jesus spoke were only clear to those who believed. The same type of understanding holds true to this day.

We tend to draft exemptions to justify our sinful desires, overlook specific text, dilute content, and focus on a favorite book that provides a means to an end. Accepting the Bible in its entirety is how your faith stands on rock-solid ground. It is how you weather the storm of doubt, come to a place of healing, and fortify your defenses against attacks. Warding off assaults from a visible enemy is easy in contrast to defending against internal assailants. Unless, that is, you've gone through spiritual combat training.

Proverbs 22:6 provides clear instructions for us to focus on raising the next generation of warriors. This verse is key to defeating PTS: "Raise a child in the way they should go..." Growing deep roots in children will help them throughout their lives. Warriors who return to their childhood roots can find healing. This biblical principle is proactive medicine. Saving heroes and raising warriors is a crucial step in healing America. It is my goal to immunize against the spiritual infection of the human condition.

My faith in a divine appointment got me through tough times. The very core of my existence was challenged. I was slowly dying because I thought my purpose was fulfilled, that I was no longer valuable. It wasn't until I heard from God that I stopped faking it and began making it. The name 10 CAN came to me in audible form when I dozed off in church. In my self-pity, I had forgotten about my calling from 2005 Rick Warren's book, *Purpose Driven Life* (2002), which would come full circle in mine.

God gives each of us time, talents, and treasure to use for His glory - and our success. Failure to use these gifts accordingly can leave us feeling empty inside. Reflecting on 2005, I recalled a fire in my soul that I could barely contain. Still serving in the military, I decided to begin exploring best practices and picked up unique missionary work. Traditional missionaries travel abroad, but I felt a conviction to serve my local community. Coaching military children, leading adventures, harvesting wild game for homeless shelters, and speaking to large military audiences is how I began 10 CAN. Taking it a step further, I started on a master's degree at Southwestern College for Youth Ministry. The road was not well traveled, and many obstacles blocked my path. I hurdled, crawled, lifted, jumped, and pulled my way forward. Somewhere along the road, I found a chainsaw and began cutting a trail for others to follow.

The way forward may seem impossible, but appearances can be deceptive. Remember, someone before you wielded a saw to clear your path. Progress depends on your ability to stand on your rock during the storm. Satisfy your desire to fight by joining forces with me. The path you seek may be your greatest challenge yet. Rest assured, your faith and family will endure if you build your house on that rock (Matthew 7:24–27).

Faith and Family

The two most common regrets on people's deathbeds are their faith and family. There are many variables that create a unique perspective. Allow me to tell a story:

Like all but one, this story begins when a man and woman have a child. The child eats, sleeps, and grows. As time passes, the child starts learning and advancing in his intellect. The child is exposed to cultural normalcies and adapts to fit in. The worldly environment challenges his inner spirit and conscientious upbringing. His promiscuous lifestyle ends when he finds the woman of his dreams. He marries and eventually fathers three children. His relationship with God was a religious obligation, which he soon felt to be irrelevant. Becoming a movie star was his dream. He soon finds little time for personal relationships, much less going to church. He grows further from God and his family and closer to the world. He lives a purposeful life but always feels something is missing. His ambitious lifestyle leads to fame and fortune, but his race comes to a halt when he is diagnosed with stage 4 lung cancer. The doctors give him less than a week to live. Dread and guilt overtake him. He laid in his hospital room with no visitors. A chaplain making his rounds visits him and asks if he has any last requests. He confesses to the chaplain that he wishes he'd done more with his family and that their absence during his end is the most devastating feeling ever. He then requests that the chaplain help him find God in hopes of offering penance for his sins. His heart is heavy with regret, and he wrestles with turmoil to make his way back. The chaplain reminds him that the gift of life isn't something we earn but freely receive. He accepts the gift and passes. Few attend his funeral. His legacy erodes with time, and his achievements are forgotten. All that he worked for is gone.

This story has been told countless times before and, unfortunately, will repeat itself many times over. It's because we're caught up in what society deems a priority and lose focus on what's profoundly important. Little value is placed on parenting. No awards are offered for the parent of the year, no accolades for being devoted to God—only hunger for negative press. There's pressure to be the best, to make rank (get a promotion), to create a legacy. None of that matters in the end. So why not leapfrog ahead and plan a regretless death? Begin living for your faith and family, and let's bridge the gap from insignificant to purposeful.

Bridging the Gap

Social gaps create division across US and around the world. Differences in social classes, masses, religion, and politics create cultural boundaries that segregate. Lack of compassionate discussion hinders bridge development. Specialized missions fill specific gaps, like caring for the homeless, saving heroes, or raising warriors. I believe that division is bridged through self-efficacy, individual responsibility, and personal ownership. We need relationships, but must learn to be relational.

Have you ever leaned on someone you love to sustain your lifestyle? Everyone needs a crutch when they injure a knee, and most of us use it as a temporary means. We work to rehabilitate so we can walk again without aid. This state of dependence is provisional. Those who forsake their independence and unnecessarily continue using crutches enable spiritual poverty. Restoring relationships and bridging gaps requires us to take account for our personal shortcomings. You must step up to persevere.

We consume unhealthy foods, then enslave ourselves to the health-care system for recovery. We expose our minds to drama and trauma, then expect psychologists to repair us. We indulge in sinful behavior and assume the Church will rejuvenate our spirits. We increase tolerances for social misfits and wonder why the "blue line" (law enforcement) is stretched so thin. We create a welfare state of mind and blame the government for enabling poverty. We have become irresponsible in our sophisticated methodology to fill gaps when the answer is quite simple.

For the sake of brevity, let's focus on the gap between the Church and our warriors: that of theological arrogance. If that doesn't bother you, then you're a leader who acknowledge the humbling truth of divine submission. If your blood pressure rose, then you should consider reflecting on your willingness to collaborate with other spiritual leaders outside your circle. The Bible has all the answers, but our method of delivery and interpretation is what has created the podium effect and "America's Great Denominational Divide" (Burke, 2019).

The podium effect occurs when a preacher, pastor, evangelist, or priest portrays a holier-than-thou image and refuses to subject him- or herself to nonreligious truths. The truth here is that a lot of religious leaders have no firsthand experience in or with combat trauma. Many of them have grown up inside the church walls, being groomed to preach. Please don't misunderstand; I am not condemning this traditional model but instead drawing a picture to breach complacency. It often takes a warrior to reach a warrior.

The great denominational divide occurs when we think ourselves more important than the other parts of the body. The escalation of new-age gospel, for example, focuses on feel-good messages. Failure to deliver the truth about hell is like helping a baby bird escape its shell. Without suffering through the struggle of birth, the newborn bird will perish. Strength comes through struggle.

You cannot gain salvation without repentance; you cannot repent without conviction; you cannot be convicted without knowledge of right and wrong; and you cannot know right from wrong without the law. The gap between God and us is the unyielding fleshly desire for freedom from the law. These rules don't interfere in our relationship with the lawmaker or law enforcer unless we're devious. We've grown convicted against the law in social conformity for convenience. Consider those who sacrifice willingly to ensure your freedom for self-indulgence.

Warriors are witnesses of battle and carry the horrors of death and destruction. Many are intolerant of the podium effect as they have seen it among military leaders. Some of these leaders got people killed and injured, while others held little regard for personal matters. Exceptional leaders recognize the need for their subordinates and maintain interactive communication.

Military leadership is an oxymoron: a dictatorship that enforces democracy. Although this sounds unacceptable, it is necessary to fulfill our mission. Sacrificing our faith, family, friends, freedom, and often our lives can make us intolerant of inconsequential matters. However, most warriors freely give to ensure that those we defend can have first-world problems. While some warriors refuse to attend church because of the podium effect, surveys show that the two main reasons are guilt and hypocritical judgment.

During a recent Purple Heart hunting revival at BC Quarter Circle Ranch in Fort White, Florida, our group sat on the back-porch fellowshipping. As the "minister," my job is to launch conversations with others in this group who are squared away. Our specialized ministry method opens doors with our warriors for healthy conversations.

One Purple Heart veteran from Georgia didn't hesitate to join our discussion. He stated that the reason he doesn't attend church is that parishioners and preachers treat him with volatility. Others in the group agreed and concluded similar reasoning. I inquisitively proposed the idea, based on my own experiences, that maybe it was self-indifference for the things he had done that manufactures this perception. I asked if he felt treated as a black sheep. He confirmed the conduct and deduced that he'd never return to church. In jest, I explained that it's too late; he was currently in church with us.

Many know the feeling of what this warrior faces. We recognize our sins and shortcomings of the cross and refute the judgment of self-righteous people. The leading solution is the saving grace of Jesus Christ, but we abstain from joining civilian assemblies because of self-persecution. It's exhausting to pretend to fit in, to be preached at, and to be expendable. Often, we're the only ones who know our true worth.

Warriors need measurable missions, objectives, and goals. We are assets, not liabilities. We itch to operate in an environment that produces results. We are the sheepdogs sitting silently in your congregation that you keep at bay. The gap that exists between the Church and warriors is a misunderstood indifference. Churches seek parishioners, sheep that will follow and freely give to their vision. Warriors seek camaraderie and a mission to expand positive change through global operations.

From the podium effect to self-persecution, we have a lot of work to do. Complacency and fear overrule our dogma. We don't trust civilians, and civilians censure warriors. To save a hero, people must risk their circles of comfort and their podiums and reject fearfulness. Lao Tzu wrote, "He who controls others may be powerful, but he who has mastered himself is mightier still" (Brainy Quotes, 2019). Giving up on church because of a bad experience is like ceasing to eat out because of a bad meal. Give it another try or change restaurants.

Mission Possible

One of my favorite movies is *Mission Impossible*. Tom Cruise—political and religious views aside—is one of my favorite actors. His character's ability to masterfully outwit the enemy, achieve extraordinary feats, and be the most valuable asset in the world keeps me on the edge of my seat. Pushing the limits and braving defeat are learned character traits. Years of mental and physical training on a thirty-acre farm in Webster, Florida, prepared me for all kind of possibilities. The odds of us finding ourselves in Tom's shoes are slim though. Instead, we often discover that our "mission impossible" exists when we face internal tyranny from traumatic experiences. Check out this list of conflicts that kicked my butt before I learned how to fight back:

- sleep deprivation
- chronic pain
- financial hardship
- broken relationships
- being treated numerically
- socially overwhelmed (traffic, activities, obligations, etc.)
- bad decisions
- inconsiderate people
- hopelessness
- sensory overload

This list is not all inclusive, but it does focus on ten real reasons people check out. These situations may feel like impossible missions to overcome. The more of this list you struggle with, the greater the feat. If you recall,

Cruise usually fights one enemy at a time, though they may all attack at once. Some of these things are within our control, and others happen without warning. If you learn to live in the now, you will find victory in the next. Yesterday's norm will never be today's reality. Finding your new normal is how you'll turn impossible to possible.

New norms are discovered by reprogramming your life. Programs provide structured outlines of functions that empower your focus. Empowerment is a product of attitude, and *attitude* equals 100 percent of life (A = 1 + T = 20 + T = 20 + I = 9 + T = 20 + U = 21 + D = 4 + E = 5 = 100). Now that you understand the power of attitude, let's discuss some programs that may help you find the new you.

Agritherapy, dirt therapy, gardening, farming, and shepherding are examples of programs that helped me trim the dead branches in my life to stimulate post-traumatic growth. There are countless agricultural metaphors in the Bible that help us grasp reality. It is the primary go-to for nonclinical rehabilitation that gives warriors control. Eating healthy, whole foods can combat chronic pain and mental chaos. It clears the mind of smog, reduces swelling, provides purpose, enables exercise, gives a sense of accomplishment, and grounds you. This program puts you in charge of your wellness and recovery. Growing or acquiring your own organic food provides a healthy dose of sustainable satisfaction.

Outdoor recreational therapy is second in the field of nonclinical remedies that foster quality of life and is, by far, my favorite tool. A love for hunting and fishing kept me motivated while deployed. It is the deepest root of my childhood. Part of growing up on the farm was having free reign to explore, hunt, fish, build forts, dig tunnels, and live adventurously. I often reminisce and share stories with my children about the good old days. Although I cannot go back, I can replicate those experiences.

No, I don't play in the dirt with Hercules action figures anymore, but I do dream of my next adventure. Often, focusing on the next mission helps me get through tough times. I look forward to my annual hunting excursion in Arizona, but sometimes I need more. Having the next adventure scheduled reduces the chance of digression.

During each of my four deployments, I dreamt of going hunting when I returned. Planning and preparing kept my light of hope in sight. I was able to stay motivated through some of the toughest times of my life because of hunting. Now, although I don't personally hunt as much as I'd like, I can share this medicine with others.

There is boundless joy in sharing my love for hunting. In a typical year, my team and I guide nearly three hundred warriors, women, and children on hunts. Providing something positive for people to focus on during struggles is how we combat hopelessness and is part of the formula for preventing suicides.

President Theodore Roosevelt proclaimed, "There is nothing man can heal that nature cannot." Those lasting words have had a profound effect on my life. In a recent study, green space was found to be a significant factor in mental health. Brigit Katz wrote that children who grow up in the great outdoors (green space) are up to 55 percent more resilient to mental health disorders than their urban counterparts (Smithsonian, 2019).

Jo Barton and Mike Rogerson discovered that green space can be used medicinally within prescribed terms. Everyone needs different doses, and if used correctly, it can reduce suicide by fifty percent. They go further to describe waterways as blue space and claim that its effectiveness is similar. "Simple exposure to natural environments is psychologically restorative and has beneficial influences on individuals' emotions and ability to reflect on life problems" (Barton & Rogerson, 2017).

Rebecca Ruiz points out that our mental health can be mysterious, elusive, and challenging to manage. Ruiz goes on to confirm data trends which show that urban residents are more than 50 percent more susceptible to suicidal ideations (poor mental health) than their rural counterparts (Mashable, 2019). It's easy to deduce that nature is medicinal, but unlike pharmaceuticals, we negate its value. We put stock in things we can control and discount the things we cannot. The very thing that makes our lives possible is unprofitable. It isn't the mission itself that is impossible; it's our ideals for gain.

While studying specialized youth ministry, I discovered a trend: emerging adults are not transitioning into adulthood until approximately thirty years old. After evaluating the aboriginal community dynamic, I found that they mandate their children to go through a rite of passage at ten years old. These children leave as liabilities and return to their community as assets.

We must draw a line in the sand for our youth and provide a moment in their lives from which they emerge as community-impact agents. Some warriors lack the rite of passage milestone. Those of you who never got this may feel that your spiritual battle is unwinnable. I assure you that all things are possible with God on your side. It doesn't matter what your background is. Everyone's story is unique, as is your interpretation of the traumatic event. Finding a program that works for you keeps hope alive, but it all depends on your will to survive.

Retreat vs. Revival

When soldiers on the battlefield hear the word *retreat*, it stimulates a response to run away. It compels them to forgo their duty to fight and can perpetuate a feeling of defeat. In today's form, a retreat describes a getaway. I've been on several retreats that offer healing, education, and escape. Numerous organizations do retreats right. However, in my experience, something was always missing.

Growing up in a small church in Linden, Florida, I both dreaded and looked forward to revivals. *Revival* is a word used in the church to describe restitution of the spirit. It happens at times when we're desperate for change but can occur anytime, anyplace. As a kid, I looked forward to revivals because I could see girls I had a crush on every day. These girls kept me excited about church. I watched as evangelists brought fire to our community and often found conviction in my reason for attending. The daily chore of listening for several hours a night was daunting, but I realized the benefit of this burden. It was and is a motivating force for good, for positive social change. This experience planted a seed in me that helped form an innovative strategy for healing warriors as an alternative to retreating.

A warrior's revival stimulates the ethos to fight. It isn't a religious thing; it's spiritual. It targets the core of all psychological problems. The best way to stop suicide is to give someone a reason to live. I coined the term *Survival Revival* to provide context for our program that treats spiritual infections through a wilderness survival challenge. The goals of our revivals are to adjust a warriors' perspective, unwind and let nature heal without outside distractions. However, these revivals are unlike what you'll find in church. We speak few words and evangelize through action. We practice living, restore purpose, and heal hidden wounds through what I call vicarious ministry.

Vicarious Ministry

The revelation of vicarious ministry occurred during our annual hunting adventure in the Appalachian Mountains of McKee, Kentucky. My cousin, and preacher of Berea Church of God, and his father, Pastor C.W. Williams, were visiting. I requested that he share the Gospel around the campfire with our guests. However, the youth had no interest in listening at the time, so we increased the volume of our conversation. This discussion began drawing in the youth and then the adults. Before long, we were all sitting around the campfire communing, fellowshipping, and ministering to one another.

Vicarious ministry is the practice of reaching people indirectly. It uses eavesdropping advantageously. Consequentially, it elicits participation: youth enlighten us on current-day temptations; warriors and hidden heroes share burdens; and healing occurs. While vicarious ministry is most effective around a campfire, its application is unrestricted. The campfire is a vital element in healing, as it naturally relaxes our demeanor (this may not be true if fire is a trigger). However, you need not wait for the perfect moment to execute vicarious ministry. You can use it on a boat, with a goat, in the rain, or on a train. You can use it in a box, with a fox, in a house, or with a mouse. Use it in an elevator, in a car, on a bus, in a park, on the phone, in prison, or at home.

Our lives are walking testimonies. Each moment matters. Ensure that every given opportunity serves a higher purpose. You are the difference between yesterday's oppression and tomorrow's freedom.

Implementing vicarious ministry works best with equally experienced individuals. It's an empathetic conversation (walk a mile in my shoes). A healthcare provider advised me to share my troubles with friends and family. I did as advised and quickly learned that this was the worst advice ever given. It caused dissension in our relationships, which ultimately led to fewer friends and barriers in the home.

Sharing with my family resulted in my wife and children manifesting signs and symptoms of PTSD. In an intense study to better understand this phenomenon, I learned about vicarious trauma. It broke my heart to see my family enlisted with me to battle my demons. I was livid and blamed providers. Requesting help was counter intuitive because at the time, no family programs were available at the time. Instead of following the path of victimology, I took action.

In 2013, I vowed to find a better way. My research and development for adolescent development transformed to focus on warrior families. Based on my research, most military and first-responder children follow in their parents' footsteps. With many current reactive treatment programs for PTSD not working, I created a proactive modality. This notion of preventive maintenance doesn't just prepare warriors for trauma; it provides self-healing afterwards.

Medication is not always necessary, but that seems to be the first step our medical community takes. This primary approach is a band-aid tactic. We are making progress, but pacification remains a concern.

Vicarious ministry is a game changer: it offers a seat at the decision-making table, allows warriors and their families to take ownership of their well-being, and empowers relationships. It restores hope, churches the unchurched, explores uncharted waters, and revitalizes life. The Warrior Bonfire Program has a saying: "Pain shared is pain divided. Joy shared is joy multiplied." This statement epitomizes vicarious ministry. We share burdens, celebrate joy, fight together, live together, and love together.

The seed of self-destruction is hatred. Dr. Martin Luther King Jr. noted that the only way to defeat hate is through love. I believe this form of resolve is something he learned from Jesus. It is an absolute! A truth that you must accept before moving forward. It is your choice, though. Doubt and get stuck, or believe and carry on.

Carry On

Asking for help can be one of the toughest challenges for a hero. It's not that we lack the self-awareness to identify our struggles; it's that we recognize the probability of being let down, scoffed at, disavowed, or considered weak. Albeit, seeking help is like calling in reinforcements: it often takes a team to overcome the enemy.

Courage is action in the face of defeat. It gives warriors the push they need to do something, but not doing something can be just as courageous. Waiting out the self-destructive spirit of suicide requires valor. Committing suicide is the enemy taking you out. Isolation in the trenches is a common feeling, but you are not alone. If you wait, someone will come. Trust me—I've been there countless times.

This cure isn't about staying out of the trenches. Instead, it's about holding your position against an overwhelming force. My family and I suffered, but you don't have to. Death is inevitable yet living is a choice. Our desire for control feeds spiritual infections. Build a team that has your six and get to living adventurously.

Some battles are won, and some are lost. Seasons come and seasons go. People will transition through your life. Don't fret when they fail to measure up or bail out when they're needed most. A reliable team will have consistency, backups, and obtainable expectations. Center yourself on God and let Him guide your team. Those closest to you will be less shaken when a storm arises, but use caution when sharing your demons with them, as vicarious trauma is a contagion. Those who have walked your mile are more likely to understand and can provide empathetic motivation. Stay focused on the now and weather the storm.

Build your house on the rock, and it'll stand strong. Reading and understanding the Bible in its entirety offers insight and foresight. It helps us identify our friends and foes. The most challenging battle is the one against a concealed enemy. All wars require you to identify an enemy. That's difficult when the difference between right and wrong are skewed.

If you don't have a solid childhood foundation when trauma strikes, then transform in your faith of Jesus Christ. Yes, it'll be much more difficult for you than for a warrior who has a squared-away childhood, but it's not inconceivable. Childhood vitality affects adult reality. We must focus on raising the next generation of warriors to be resilient against spiritual infections. In joining this mission, you may find path to a purpose. Push forward at any pace by any means, and you'll eventually discover freedom.

In your pursuit to make a difference and leave a legacy, remember that faith and family are the two greatest regrets on one's deathbed. It doesn't matter what you achieve or the things you acquire—it will all pass away. Recognize that your family is your legacy and that your faith ensures perseverance beyond death. The challenge of overcoming the obstructive views of society can prove divergent. The world doesn't measure success accurately. A large gap between the classes and masses adds dimensional discord. It is difficult to bridge the gap between race, religion, gender, economics, and culture when we have a singular perspective.

Some of us are keen on speaking but lack the constitution to listen. The gap between warriors and the Church exists because warriors and preachers are both fraught with purpose and experiences. It is inconceivable for battle-hardened warriors to surrender without a fight. An impossible mission stimulates the warrior ethos. The Church wants warriors to surrender, but there is some confusion on that ground.

Resigning in the spiritual sense does not mean defeat. Quite the contrary! When warriors yield spiritually, their souls become part of an elite force that fights the hidden enemy. Retreating is not an option, so never give up ground (unless necessary to regroup). Instead, join a revival to stimulate post-traumatic growth. Don't wait till your deathbed to realize what's important. Live life's greatest adventure—live you.

A-TEAM

G rowing up watching B. A. (Mr. T.), Murdock, Hannibal, and Faceman on the TV show *A-Team* taught me that every person holds a unique talent. Assemble those talents for a specific mission and watch what happens. The A-Team's fight against injustice created a deep-seated desire to become an impact agent. Their ability to navigate around bureaucratic processes and legalistic boundaries was a developmental factor for me. As children, my older brother, our cousin, and I would convoy around our farm seeking and destroying the "enemy." In our make-believe world, we dug foxholes and tunnels, built forts and sniper perches, and ambushed any foes that crossed our path. We tormented family and friends, but as time went on, things changed.

When my father left, he took part of our childhood with him. His absence required us to step up sacrificially. Farm life shifted from desire to duty. Few kids enjoy doing chores on their time off but putting food on the table was something I found fulfilling. As an up-and-coming man, there was something about being a provider that was gratifying. Picking blueberries, mowing lawns, pulling weeds, raking, and feeding livestock weren't as appealing as hunting, fishing, and foraging. I don't mind hard work but being relevant now is a vital part of my existence.

Individualism is important for team cohesion. Everyone's role and value are measurable. All members of a team are accountable to one another, but most importantly, to themselves. We function here on earth as an assembly of one—humankind. As team humanity, our mission is to care for the planet and one another. We are individually responsible for our part in the unit and will be exclusively accountable for our actions. If you think you're irrelevant, then consider this: a million dollars cannot exist without a penny. You matter!

Farmers, like good parents, do not receive the props they deserve. A significant portion of institutionalized academia shuns agriculture, often leading students to believe that farming is for the less intelligent. That isn't the case. Farmers must have unrelenting patience (something many of us lack). They must have intellectual capability in science, biology, anatomy, math, language, networking, meteorology, economics, and technology. They must be physically fit to perform rigorous tasks in both good and bad weather. Lastly, farmers must be purpose driven. The characteristics that we desperately need for personal growth are epitomized in farming.

Each member of the A-Team is instrumental in the overall mission. They have common ground in the purpose of their assembly. But what if they bid for power to lead the team? Would their individual aspirations negatively impact the mission? I believe they would be rendered ineffective by the cultural manipulation that diminishes the importance of followership.

As of 2019, the average age of farmers is in their sixties. Organizations like Farmer Veteran Coalition are intervening in the impending food crisis by recruiting military veterans into the field of food sustainability. In pursuit of creating a more intelligent nation, academia has developed dependent citizens. If you cannot hunt, fish, forage, or farm, then you may be dependent on government control. In my opinion, farmers and parents are the two most important jobs on the planet. Without farmers, we would starve, and without parents, we wouldn't have farmers.

Being a parent is like taking a nonstop ride on Disney's Space Mountain. There are times to relax and enjoy smooth sailing, but then out of nowhere, you get jolted with the reality that you're on a roller coaster. You're in the dark most of the time, trying to figure things out on the fly. The onslaught of twists and turns and ups and downs often hinders your emotional stability. When you think you see a glimmer of light, it quickly fades away. Only the bravest mothers and fathers stay on the ride. The weak get out and run away, sometimes coming back when it's convenient for them.

Parents are farmers of children. They must be informed, loving, nurturing, educational, a mentor, defender, and protector, and be willing to selflessly sacrifice everything. But there is a parental anomaly occurring in America. Many parents are not taking the necessary steps to prepare their children to launch on time. The average emerging adult is living at home with parents until they are around thirty years old.

My oldest daughter left home on her eighteenth birthday. She took flight—not because my house isn't loving or accepting, but because she was ready. I believe that a rite of passage (ROP) sets families up for success. I developed a ROP that is a wilderness survival challenge which allows youth a transitional platform into productive resilient adulthood. Children build confidence and discover new possibilities, while parents witness their child's potential.

It was difficult to let my daughter go, but in the face of self-doubt, I realized that my investment into her preparedness had not been in vain. The ROP we did in 2012 at Roosevelt Lake in Arizona taught her resilience and grit. Hitching a ride on a boat to the other side of the lake, we jumped out into the water and worked our way to shore. We slept under the open stars on a sandy beach with wild cattle lurking nearby. I mysteriously caught a largemouth bass with my bare hand a hundred yards offshore (true story). My daughter learned to use resources wisely, reduce exposure, and pace herself. She also learned to signal for rescue when the time was right. We did a second ROP down the Santa Fe River, surviving with only the food and water we acquired in the field. A surprise party awaited her at the finish line at Poe Springs Park, Florida.

Capitalizing on opportunities to teach can develop situational awareness. Camping in inclement weather, thriving without electricity, or running water, and evading hostile encounters with illegal immigrants on the border has fostered an appreciation for the now. However, the most significant thing I taught her has been spiritual empowerment: that which gives life in death. It is the light in darkness, the calm in the storm, the peace that passes all understanding.

My duty to prepare her for launch meant sacrificing personal desires. Parents who do this for their children discover that their temporary inconvenience is an investment in their legacy. Don't just send your kids off to camp and expect results. Learn how to cultivate the seeds that are planted.

If you recall the A-Team dynamic, Hannibal was the parental element. He provided direction and guidance. His leadership served the team well. He leaned on team members to fulfill the mission by using their skills accordingly. Likewise, fathers are divinely appointed to be the head of the household (Ephesians 5:22–33), and mothers are often the glue that holds the family together. One without the other can create hardship. However, it's worth clarifying that divorce is necessary in specific situations.

The concern I have is adults trumping their duty as parents with their desires as individuals. I hypothesize that because we've removed the glamour from devoted parenthood, we've created a plaque of self-serving individuals. When parents commit to their children they function more synergistically for a greater purpose as a family unit. My dedication as a parent led my daughter to write several poems to me. I recently found this one dated July 20, 2012:

> Dad,
> I love you more than you love honey,
> I love you more than mom loves money,
> I love you more than Adina loves rice,
> For your love does not come with a price.
> You never flee,
> For you love me,
> I've met forks in the road,
> But you've been so bold,
> To sweep tears off my face,
> And to drain guilt from this place.
> That is why I love you so,
> There is more, though,
> But I must go…

There are no words to describe the joy parents experience when they get it right and no horror worse than when our children go wrong. There are no accolades to recognize a parent sufficiently for a job well done, yet we're quick to throw stones when a child goes astray. Like farmers putting food on your table, parents grow community impact agents. May they become your friends, neighbors, firefighters, paramedics, police officers, preachers, tradespeople, soldiers, educators, truck drivers, and many other valuable members of America. Most of all, may they remember their parents' sacrifices for their success.

Our precursors can shape who we are, but they don't control our actions. It is for us to decide our positions on the team. You get out what you put in. So sharpen your skills, tighten your laces, saddle up, and warrior on.

Impact vs. Liability

Becoming an impact agent is easier than you think, but so is being a liability. You can be both, but wouldn't that be hypocritical? Or is it? In my youth, many memories were made on family vacations. One year we took a road trip to the Florida Keys, and my father brought his boat, scuba gear, and fishing poles. We headed out to a spot my father selected. He tossed out the anchor, hoisted the dive flag, and began gearing himself and my brother up for the lobster hunt. I grabbed my fishing pole, put a leader on it, and baited it with shrimp. As my brother and father began their descent, I cast my line.

Mom and my sister were enjoying the sun and a fresh breeze, until they both got seasick. I was catching fish left and right, which helped me ignore their moaning and projectile vomiting. After a while, my father and brother emerged from the depths about two hundred yards away. Dad yelled for Mom to bring the boat over, but she was too ill to move. He continued yelling and screaming, then held up a lobster to get her attention. I heard and saw him loud and clear and wanted to help, but he had never taken the time to teach me how to work the vessel. I was young and treated dismissively. He saw me only as a liability and not an asset, but I had a cooler full of fish.

As time passed, I too began to recognize my youthfulness as a liability. I did foolish things, lost focus of priorities, and made poor decisions. However, when I was counted on to bring home sustenance, I delivered. The difference between someone being a liability and being impactful is having a purpose. It was fulfilling to take care of my own; it gave me a reason for existing. And that's what people need. But what happens when you're no longer needed?

My mom worked diligently to overcome countless barriers and single-handedly led our family out of poverty. My father saw her as a liability, but when he left, she stepped up and quickly filled his shoes. Susceptible people tend to reflect the way they are treated. I posit that children and youth are liabilities because that's how adults treat them. I could've easily driven the boat over to my father had he believed in me enough to invest the time to train me.

Bringing wild game home proved my worth to my mom, but that wasn't enough. One of the essential elements in life couldn't shake the social norm of treating me as a liability. In my vulnerable state, I reverted to self-indulgences and compromising behavior—typical adolescence. The window of opportunity to further develop my responsibility slipped away because nobody recognized my potential. My A-Team wasn't using me to my full ability, and it wasn't until I joined the military that I felt purposeful.

The US military can extract the greatest potential from its members. Not everyone measures up, though, and some don't make the cut. Those who do become global impact agents. People from all walks of life find fulfillment and commonality in duty. We learn that being a liability could jeopardize our brothers and sisters in arms. Our mission has little to do with the big picture and everything to do with those we love. We go to great lengths in service to our country. Some of us experience the worst humanity has to offer. Many witness it from afar, and some leave unscathed. Those who are directly impacted by a traumatic experience may incur PTS. Those witnessing trauma indirectly can experience PTS symptoms, but I propose it to be secondary traumatic stress (STS).

In working on my dissertation for traumatized law enforcement officers, I discovered the difference between PTS and STS. Both are showstoppers if not treated properly. Treatments don't always need counseling or medications, though that's the first thing our medical community throws at them. There are a variety of ways to overcome these mental health "challenges" and continue moving forward. Most leaders view individuals with PTSD as liabilities, and few even know about STS. These traumatic experiences can create vulnerabilities, but they also create opportunities for growth.

Correctly handled, a traumatic experience can enhance a person's value. It takes a Hannibal-type leader to extract a warrior's potential following a traumatic experience. Being a seasoned warrior comes at a cost. Those who dig in and fortify their foxhole allows the enemy to surround them. Playing defense means an attack is always imminent. Holding your ground until reinforcements arrive is a temporary solution. You must eventually take the fight to the enemy. Don't let people convince you that you're a liability. You're a warrior!

Battle Cry

A famous thirteenth-century battle ensued as Scotland desired independence from England's tyrannical rule. An open field was the last stand, as Mel Gibson reenacted the role of William Wallace in the movie *Braveheart* (1995). Hollywood did an exceptional job capturing my attention as Wallace courageously led the battle. With his face painted blue, Gibson delivered a memorable speech to his brothers in arms. What followed was one of the most significant battle cries ever heard (in my opinion).

Wearing out the edge of my seat, I became so engulfed in the theatrics that I was ready to join the Scottish rebellion and take back our motherland. I was even willing to give my life for this cause. It's incredible how a battle cry can generate such a compelling thought. Some of you reading this have heard a warrior release such a roar in combat and can verify its spiritual motivation. Although Gibson may have never faced a real war, he has inspired many warriors to fight for freedom.

Many of us face inner tyranny that becomes our oppressor. Cruel thoughts, provocative visions, horrific nightmares, hypervigilance, anxiety, anger, and frustration torment our minds. The external tyrants who view us as dangerous and restrict our freedoms add to the problem. They tax us, steal inheritances, hijack innovation, and bombshell our motivation. Often, people we entrust with our vulnerabilities abandon us. It's time to unleash the warrior within—the warrior you've been holding back because others want to tame you.

The spirit of reason, meaning, and purpose provides emotional satisfaction. It's how you feel after fighting a good battle and the gratification of being needed. You're the one who makes the A-Team what it is. You belong here, now, in this moment. So let out your battle cry and live fearlessly.

My purpose shifted after combat injuries and a medical retirement. I believe that God was preparing me for a top-tier leadership position to influence military policies through a Christian perspective. I was racing through the ranks and being groomed for the Pentagon. But on that fateful day in September, at the foothills of the Himalayas, it all changed. What I thought was the end was just the beginning.

It didn't dawn on me for quite some time that my training was still taking place. Superior to a promotion to our military headquarters was an advancement to discipleship—an impossibility while in uniform. I would no longer be working for a single country but for the Kingdom that encompasses all nations, all planets, all of everything. I serve at the pleasure of God Almighty; get paid in joy, peace, and freedom; and have a team that is always there with a boss that brings out the best. My mission is to generate a movement to save heroes, raise warriors, and restore hope.

The A-Team was an elite group of men assembled for actional change. My team looks remarkably similar. The only requirements for joining are that you bring your best, that you do not retreat or surrender, and that you accept God as your commander. We're going to war with the hidden enemy. It's time to train, plan, and execute our duties as warriors. It's time to cast out self-destructive thoughts, realize our value, and release a thunderous battle cry that unites our allies in Christ. Who's ready for spiritual combat training?

Why Me?

Have you ever asked yourself that question? Sure you have, and so have I. But the real question is, "Why not me?" If I'm "fearfully and wonderfully made" (Psalm 139:14), then why do I keep getting the short end of things? Before God formed you in the womb, He knew you. Before you were born, He consecrated you (Jeremiah 1:5). I'm here to deliver a message of hope, peace, and joy; to free you from the burden of things you've done; and to reignite your purpose. You and I are loved unconditionally. Take courage, my friend, and let's get back your life.

It is a life of reason and meaning - a life worth living for a death worth dying. Everyone's time expires. Only when you accept this reality can you escape self-imprisonment. It is the one thing that can overcome the fear of death and motivate you to pay the ultimate price—willingly, for a cause.

Do you feel lost, trapped, or drowned out by the multitude? Is your path on a dead-end road? Are you wondering why you're still alive? Do you feel that you have been treated numerically in health care, religion, politics, or work? You're not alone, and you're not wrong. Our society has become caught up in the numbers game. We want measurable outcomes and data. We're driven by a biased definition of *success* and count what others deem to be successful as our own. This popular opinion is misleading. The number of people who attend an event, total number of likes on a post, and the number of patients we see in a day are worldly depictions of success. Defining success through this culture of quantitative leadership isn't always factual. Qualitative leaders do not keep count. These impact agents have a spiritual accountant doing it for them.

Counting may not be enjoyable, but it's how stakeholders measure success. It is an uncomfortable necessity to ensure mission continuation and growth. Being a catalyst for salvation is what stimulates my energy source. I am inspirationally driven by Desmond Doss's famous prayer on Hacksaw Ridge: "Lord, just one more." One person can make a difference by joining the right team that utilizes his or her unique talents to provoke qualitative effectiveness.

"Attention to Orders" is a statement read to a formation of troops snapping them into position, to recognize an individual for heroic action. Many warriors have experienced this, but few have been on the receiving end. The difference between the formation at attention and the individual on stage is nothing more than opportunity. Most have what it takes to brave a situation, but you must first master fight or flight. Until you've been in a situation, you cannot predict how you'll act. You can only physically, mentally, and spiritually prepare yourself.

Role-play is an effective training method. Think through situations before they occur so that you can create muscle memory to overcome flight tendencies. Spiritually prepare by grasping the concept of this book. I train for conditions that include combat, mishaps, fire, survival, medical emergencies, hostile encounters, and disasters. Each situation tests mental, physical, and spiritual fortitude. Some things are unpredictable, but preparedness helps even the odds.

In 2007, while serving as an Air Force recruiter, I encountered a life-or-death situation. While I was following a school bus full of Air Force Junior Reserve Officer Training Course (AFJROTC) cadets for a weekend camp, I witnessed a black Mustang overcompensate to dodge the bus while coming around the curve of the rural back road we were on. In my rearview mirror, I saw the car overturn and roll multiple times. I hit the brakes and reversed my government-issued vehicle to the place I had last seen the car. I quickly followed the skid marks to a sharp cliff, where I found the vehicle—wheels still turning. Without hesitation I descended to check on the driver. With only passenger side access, I entered the mangled vehicle to render aid. The driver was semi-conscious, but alive. His legs were pinned under the steering wheel and he appeared to have a punctured lung. He was in critical condition and on the edge of death. Without cell reception I was unable to call 911, but fortunately another vehicle soon arrived with a group of guys who went for help.

In my effort to stabilize the man, I revived him into a state of awareness, but he responded in violence. He took a swing without striking me then attempted to bite me. He then fell unconscious. Nearly thirty minutes passed before the first volunteer firefighter arrived. She knew the guy and was too shaken to take command, so I put her behind him to stabilize his C-spine. I acquisitioned her radio and began calling in resources and directing emergency responders.

After it all was said and done, I continued to the camp. Upon arrival, the AFJROTC chief asked me what happened. The people on the bus hadn't witnessed the crash, but the chief saw that my uniform was a mess. After explaining to him what had taken place, he offered me a chance to clean up and debrief. After changing outfits and cleaning off glass, blood, and dirt, I got back to my original mission. I didn't think anything else of it until six months later, when my commander invited me to the front stage during a conference in Nashville, Tennessee. Here's what I received:

DEPARTMENT OF THE AIR FORCE

THIS IS TO CERTIFY THAT

THE AIR FORCE COMMENDATION MEDAL

HAS BEEN AWARDED TO

STAFF SERGEANT MATTHEW R. BURKE

FOR

ACT OF COURAGE
18 MAY 2007

ACCOMPLISHMENTS

Staff Sergeant Matthew R. Burke distinguished himself by an act of courage on 18 June 2007. On that date, Sergeant Burke observed a horrific automobile accident in Owen County, Kentucky. Immediately without concern for his own personal safety, Sergeant Burke scaled a 10-foot embankment to render aid to the injured driver. Once on the scene, he instructed a bystander to call 911 while he entered the mangled vehicle. He found the driver with a chest wound, crushed lower extremities, rapid breathing, and a weak rapid pulse. While providing first aid, Sergeant Burke was able to stabilize the driver for 30 minutes until emergency medical service arrived. In addition, he assisted with the Jaws of Life and helped extract the victim from the wreckage. Sergeant Burke's bravery and decisive actions are credited with assisting in saving the young man's life. By his prompt action and humanitarian regard for his fellow man, Sergeant Burke has reflected credit upon himself and the United States Air Force.

GIVEN UNDER MY HAND
25 OCTOBER 2007

MICHAEL D. BRICE, Colonel, USAF
Commander, 367th Recruiting Group

Special Order: G-19 Condition: 0 PAS: CO8W3ZF RDP: 21 Aug 07
AF FORM 2224, JUL '80

My response to the wreck had not been courageous in my mind. I was simply doing my civic duty because I was in the right place at the right time to exercise my training. Had I been complacent or unprepared, I wouldn't have known to call in air support to medevac the driver. The helicopter arrived shortly after the first responders. Their promptness and expertise are what really saved that guy's life.

I share this with you because it's an integral part of my point. I was a valuable member of the Air Force. Some leaders are qualitative, and some are quantitative. The leaders who took the time to recognize my actions were qualitative and inspired me to give more. I felt individually valuable.

My efforts reflect nothing more than what anyone else in that room would have done at that moment. It provided a much-needed answer to my question, "Why me?"

Ethical behavior and daily acts of courage receive little recognition. Special attention isn't what good guys seek, but it's a nice perk of our contributions to humanity. On the other hand, many bad guys are products of attention. They feed off publicity, the reputation, and the thrill of living on the edge. What they don't realize is that they cannot fill that void on their own. Only one thing can satisfy their craving- salvation.

We're facing one of the greatest plagues to ever sweep across the globe, and the only medicine that will stop this outbreak is love. "Why me" is relevantly irrelevant. It is essential to know what your purpose is, but it is more important to live like you have a mission, even when you're in doubt. Fake it until you make it!

Subject matter experts (SMEs) have identified a variety of reasons for school shootings. Some profess that they happen because we've removed God from the schools. Some SMEs claim it's because we don't allow parents to discipline like they used to, while others state that video games have desensitized our youth. The list of reasons continues with valuable and accurate points, but I would like to add some intricate thought. What if the solution is a singularity? Not a conjuncture of false reasoning introduced by agenda-driven, constitution-violating, anti-patriotic enemies of the state, but rather an isolated demise of morality.

Those who lack restraint are irrationally impulsive and often suffer from an identity crisis and a broken moral compass. These misfits cause social chaos and are disruptive, destructive, and disgraceful. They lack purpose and believe in misguided truths. They are spiritually infected and suffer under the thinking of, "What's in it for me?" Personal gain and gratification haunt their minds. Although, there are anomalies. These are inherently good people who are lost in the crowd and don't know how to be found. They are infected. There is good news, though: your phone is ringing, and God is on the other end. He knows your why and wants to guide you to it. But it is up to you to answer the call. Let it continue ringing and wallow in self-pity or answer and rise to the occasion.

As a child, I felt unique, like I had some grand purpose in my life. I wanted to fit in and stand out at the same time. Most adults grouped me in with my peers. The concept of team threaded all parts of my life, and it felt like my individual purpose was irrelevant. I tried outperforming others to be the best, but no matter how hard I worked, it was never enough. I felt expendable.

It wasn't until God's revelation on my life that I understood the reason for my existence. I had sought attention all my life to be different and have a chance to stand out among my peers, but the challenge of singularity is recognizing your importance to the Kingdom. You may be required on the big stage like Reverend Billy Graham, or you may be needed on a battlefield.

In a time of instant gratification, it is challenging to wait your turn. Although patience is a virtue, I add that it reveals your purpose as well. It is one of the reasons why I use hunting as a method of adolescent development.

God has a plan for your life; wait for its revelation. You can impact thousands of lives by allowing your virtue to grow with time. Saving lives through spiritual heroism changes countless lives through unmeasurable influence. You are an irreplaceable member of the team. Whether it's a team of one or one hundred, acting courageously under fire gives life a chance.

Action Beyond Prayer

Many of us have heard someone say, "I'll pray for you." But what does this mean? Among believers, it is a slogan of hope. Though these four words cite truth in casting our burdens upon our Maker, they have been watered down by shallow friendliness, as if your troubles can be magically washed away with rainbows and roses. It often means that the person who says it doesn't have the desire or time to invest in your situation—a cookie-cutter Christian response that may or may not be genuine. Praying can be an easy out. Unfortunately, it can also portray a holier-than-thou attitude. "I'll pray for you" is often an inaction, the opposite of how warriors operate.

Warriors act and expect the same in return. Empty promises result in a disconnection. "I'll pray for you" means nothing without follow-through. In my experience, many people speak meaninglessly. It is a farce for self-fulfillment. Weeding through believers to find the few who will go the distance can be disheartening. This can drive warriors into isolation. Empty promises are detrimental to the Church because they deter believers who are action-oriented and fill the pews with self-indulgent followers.

Please hear my heart, believers, and spiritual leaders: pray <u>with</u> us because we need it, but deep dive or stay ashore. We expect you to go beyond prayer and keep your promises. Prayer is the most potent weapon we have. I'm asking you to use it with precision to make a difference in our lives. Go a step further than prayer, though. God uses us to be His hands and feet, to get things done. Connect with me if you want to help save a hero.

Warriors, my brothers and sisters in arms, listen up. You have a responsibility. Just because you took off the uniform, unlaced your boots, and are adjusting to civilian life doesn't mean you have to become a sheep. Don't lower your expectations of people, as mental health specialists might suggest. Instead, find those who show themselves worthy of your friendship. Beware, though—you will get disappointed. Your expedition to locate someone who measures up may feel hopeless. In testing potential friends, realize that you, too, have flaws. It's okay to befriend someone who is also overcoming brokenness, but be sure you balance each other out. Sharpen each other, don't fuel one another's self-destruction.

To gain friends, you must show yourself friendly; to gain trust, you must prove yourself trustworthy; to gain respect, you must take responsibility for your life. At some point in time, we will all find ourselves in need. It's okay to ask for help but note my advice to spiritual leaders—be precise. Countless programs exist to support to you. No matter what your problem is, there's a solution. If you don't ask, we'll never know.

Becoming vulnerable is not a tactically sound maneuver. However, it is a necessary step in the healing process. It's not advisable to let everyone see your vulnerability, nor should you remain in this state. Find the right friend, join the right team, and strive for righteousness (1 Timothy 6:11). Don't fret if it's slow going. Your life isn't a social media platform or the instantaneously gratifying internet. It is a clock, ticking away one second at a time, one heartbeat at a time, one breath at a time. Your job is to take one step at a time.

In each precious moment, remember—you are here and now for a reason. Your salvation is paid in full, so there's nothing for you to earn.

However, you know good and well that just sitting back and doing nothing is not in your nature. You want to charge the enemy, brave the flames, and carry the cross. You may yearn for an opportunity to die for a cause. Few things are worse than dying in vain. In times of despair, when you want it to just stop, is when you're at your moment of glory.

Falling to your knees and surrendering your soul to God is not weakness. It is your action beyond prayer, your chance to join the most elite fighting force this world has ever known, your time of redemption. To fight on requires spiritual surrender. Find someone who will act beyond prayer, and you'll discover your spiritual medic (James 5:16).

The Bible says that every knee shall bow and every tongue confess that Jesus Christ is Lord (Isaiah 45:23; Romans 14:11; Philippians 2:10–11). Even the hardest of hearts have been broken and mended through love and prayer. Praying is the one thing that everyone can do to make a difference. It isn't always about other people, though. Prayer can set us free from the burden of defeat. By praying for those who oppose you, cause you harm, or seek to destroy you, you become the guard and not the prisoner.

"Faith without works is dead" (James 2:26). Many Christians believe humans are incapable of earning salvation—and for good reason (Titus 3:5–7). While this is true, it can be used as justification for laziness. Jesus ordered us to go and do. We, as believers, receive a commission in the book of Mark, chapter 16 verse 15. We have marching orders to deploy and carry out a mission. Jesus was a man of action, and He expects the same of us.

Anatole France wrote, "All changes, even the most longed for, have their melancholy; for what we leave behind us is a part of ourselves; we must die to one life before we can enter another." Easier said than done! Before my injury, I played sports with my children. My emotional composition was steadfast, and my focus on them never waned. Finding the new norm in my life took persistence, courage, and defeat. I surrendered what I could no longer be for that which I was becoming. I tend to be insensitive as a form of compartmentalization. Most spiritual leaders, civilians, family members, neighbors, and superficial friends disapprove. What they don't see is all the hard work that went into building these calluses—the journey through perdition.

My effort to remain in control put me on a path of destruction. It wasn't until I shifted perspective that I found freedom. I infused my life with action and made my future, my hope, and my love happen through practice. I honor my Creator through purpose—not by passively waiting for His grace, but by doing what I can to make things happen right now, here on earth (Bradley Whitford). Helen Keller put it best: "Security is mostly a superstition. It does not exist in nature, nor do the children of men as a whole experience it. Avoiding danger is no safer in the long run than outright exposure. Life is either a daring adventure or nothing."

This concept frees you from the fear of death and overcomes your desire for control. People who lose self-control because they panic, reveal a dirty secret. Flopping, flailing, screaming, or freezing is a form of internal anguish. People panic because they fear death, but in so doing increase the odds of dying. Restraint, or lack thereof, is also a spiritual infection that produces certain types of crazy.

A person panicking while drowning will often need to be subdued before rescue, otherwise he or she may drown the rescuer. Knocking someone into reality is like the military "shock and awe" campaigns. John Steinbeck points out that a "sad soul can kill quicker than an infection." Sadness occurs when we compare what is to what was, or to what could be. Action beyond prayer is akin to the Air Force core value "service before self." Praying creates submission and prepares you to rescue a panicking soul. Be the shock and awe and put others first.

Service Before Self

The greatest demonstration of love is to lay down your life for a friend (John 15:13). Sacrificing yourself is often translated literally, but I would argue that it has been misconstrued. Many believe sacrifice to be more valuable than obedience; taking a bullet for your partner, diving on a grenade for your team, or running into an explosive inferno for strangers are examples of the price some heroes pay. However, there are other ways for us to show our love for one another. Serving sacrificially is a similar form of heroism.

Since childhood, I have dreamed of dying a heroic and worthy death. This hero complex was buried in my teen years when it became all about me. After Jasmine's inception, it resurfaced. I realized that having a noble death requires positioning for a heroic moment. In so doing, I underwent training to become a firefighter and emergency medical technician.

Serving in fire-rescue provided fulfillment in my life. It became more than I bargained for, though, and less than I expected. There was no training that mentally prepared me for the things I saw. No counseling or debriefings— just endure and press forward. But I loved it and found myself needing something more.

Visiting the Air Force recruiter, Sergeant Michael Fly in Leesburg, Florida, led me to an extraordinary change. The military provided everything that I desired: equitable promotions, moral rules and regulations, global purpose, and an opportunity to die for a cause. Thirteen years of service and four deployments delivered several close calls. God had other plans for me, though—plans to prosper me.

When my military career came to a stern halt, my mind went astray. The heroic legacy I yearned for was stripped from me; only remnants of things I had done and seen remained. It wasn't until my deep dive into the Bible that I discovered God's plan on my life. His expectations and straightforward directions provoked a new me. I embellished that hero complex with obedience in service rather than dutiful sacrifice.

Volunteering more than sixty hours a week in a charitable setting empowered my purpose. I gave freely of my time, talent, and treasure because I love helping people. The pleasure I gain from creating happiness in others is euphoric. It triumphs over naysayers and haters, skeptics, scandals, and pharisees. Love conquers all, and you don't have to die to demonstrate sacrificial love. As a matter of fact, God prefers obedience to sacrifice (1 Samuel 15:22). Giving freely of your life, in obedience to your duty, instigates love that manifests peace and joy. But what about the style of love that only battle-hardened warriors know?

There are those among us who hold the line between tyranny and freedom—warriors. Some refer to them as sheepdogs. Not everyone in law enforcement or the military fits the bill, though. To be a warrior or a sheepdog, one must be equipped to fight. They must have a combative spirit that will, without hesitation, lead them to sacrifice their self for the greater good. Warriors draw fire, dive into a foxhole to rescue a buddy, and run toward danger. They do not count themselves worthy but will pay the ultimate price without hesitation.

Warriors epitomize our definition of heroism and regard their lives as a living sacrifice for others. They are duty-bound, obedient to a cause, and loyal to one another. They are rough around the edges and loved by few.

God sees you, warrior. He understands you. He loves you. Your sacrifice is worthy of a heavenly salute but only if it's not in vain. Death in love is a connection with God. According to 1 John 5:3, if you know love, you know God because God is love. While it's notable that God desires obedience over sacrifice, I believe He honors the warrior who pays it all.

Service before self cannot succeed without the self. You must gain position before you can be of use. Popularity is, unfortunately, a part of the process of representing an organization. People need a face to connect to a cause. The Wounded Warrior Project uses service members who have visible impairments to grab your attention. The American Cancer Society uses patients who have suffered the worst surgeries to showcase evidence of their progress. Saint Jude's Hospital presents the reality of suffering children. Many donors give quite generously to these well-deserving missions and other similar causes because they see a need that trumps their own. They obey an emotional stimulation to sacrifice their hard-earned money so that others may have a fighting chance. Like the face of an organization that plays its part, the donor is instrumental in funding the service.

Growing up in sports taught me to be competitive. Once I stopped playing, I began coaching. I follow the coaching strategies of those men in my life who impacted me the greatest, but I got it wrong. Carrying a losing streak, I held my head high, knowing that my utmost goal was positively influencing youth to become better citizens. I sought to befriend them to ensure they knew that they had someone in their corner. What I didn't realize is that I had failed them as a coach.

The premise of coaching didn't dawn on me until recently. As a father of two amazing daughters, I pride myself in getting parenting right—so much so that I invest countless hours studying best parenting practices and then repackaging for application. I lost over three years with my family, so taking the opportunity to invest time happens without hesitation. Creating a nonprofit allowed me to continue serving with them at my side.

Often, I would force my daughters to make up after a fight. Their harmonious relationship means everything to me because they are my legacy. In my endeavor to be the greatest dad in the world, I selfishly fostered a cohesive relationship between father and daughter, just like my young athletes. What I should have done was to be the coach/dad who creates a bond through common ground.

As an athlete, I never understood why I had to run when someone else messed up. It was unfair, and I began to despise my coach. But like in the movie *Facing the Giants*, we began to function as a team unit and won countless games. The coach never explained himself as I thought he should, but now I get it. As a father, I have succeeded in maintaining a relationship between myself and my daughters, but I failed the bigger picture. A wedge in our relationship may have created more common ground in their relationship. This commonality forges bonds. As a father, I balance their success with my love and affection. After all, their relationship with each other is the legacy that will live on after I'm gone.

Every team needs a leader, followers, and loyalty between the two. Warriors in the grind of recovery should recognize their need for a team. Those who don't may find themselves in a destructive pattern. For most, being the Hannibal of their squad is the goal. Stripping them of that is like reducing a hunting dog to a house pet.

Warriors need to know that real people exist in churches, in their communities, and in their circles. Commit loyalty to a warrior, and you'll discover a relentless friend. Cheat them with empty promises and shallow talk, and you may never gain their trust again. To each their own, but for warriors, we are one. We coexist to ensure humankind thrives beyond the self-destructive nature. Our greatest desire is for peace. Most of us resonate with Mr. T, who pities the fool that messes with our team.

Team Members

Millions of people spend billions of dollars for some things that are completely free. Purpose and pleasure can be found in our present position. It's a mindset that creates the euphoric experiences - a personal utopia. The purest form of happiness comes from within. Being a productive member of a team and giving freely of yourself can induce such a feeling. There must be balance and reasonable expectations, though. Most of this book focuses on the warrior, but I believe it is essential to highlight others on the team.

Hidden Heroes

Wives, husbands, and intimate friends play a significant role. We rely on you for moral support. You are a Hidden Hero (coined by the Elizabeth Dole foundation) who draws fire to ensure we stay the course of recovery. You are on the frontline of our spiritual war. It's important that you don't get caught in crossfire or become a victim of friendly fire.

Exposure can result in cognitive trauma, especially when you're emotionally involved. Correlated with PTS, many spouses suffer from vicarious trauma (VT). VT produces signs and symptoms of PTSD, but it's not the same. Nor is it treated the same. You didn't experience the trauma, but you're often the metaphorical punching bag of those who have. You provide overwatch, support the command center, run the chow hall, conduct third-country national duty, manage logistics, transport, mediate, and satisfy our fleshly desires. You selflessly bear the burdens of war.

VT will wear you down, burn you out, and tear you apart if you don't have outside support. Being a Hidden Hero is a thankless job, but for those who pass the test of time, it is a rewarding investment. For those who cannot handle it, don't receive the necessary support, or are overcome by VT, the feeling of hostility can arise.

Healing happens at home! You are the key player. Healthcare and other service organizations are beginning to recognize you as an integral part of holistic wellness. Good leadership sees you as part of the team, but most don't realize your significance yet. There is little support across the country for you, but I hope to change that. Stay the course, unless you're facing abuse. Find a church and get your warrior pointed in the right direction. Connect with a mission like the Christian Adventure Network to combat VT and strengthen resilience. You are not alone!

God will carry you when you're weak, pick you up when you fall, and comfort you when you're hurt. He'll provide for you when you have nothing, help you overcome traumatic thoughts, and give you rest. Your mission is impossible without Him. Lean not on your own understanding (Proverbs 3:5–6).

Although you may not fully grasp what your hero is going through, empower them with empathy (tough love), don't enable with sympathy. Do not instigate a fight to stimulate an emotional response. It may be gratifying to you, but it could end catastrophically. Know your physical abilities and keep it simple. Verbal judo is suitable for de-escalation but bad for arguing. Be mindful of your warriors' triggers. Try to get in sync.

It can be difficult to explain certain things, especially with a TBI (Traumatic Brain Injury). Anticipating our thoughts, feelings, and desires creates intimacy and cohesion. We shouldn't expect you to be a tactical operator, but sometimes we unfairly do. Some warriors need a battle buddy who can swiftly move from point to point, covering our six, twelve, three, and nine.

Communication can be difficult when our mind gets entangled with chaos. A TBI can disrupt the flow of thought. With PTSD there is a thin line between friend and foe. Help us maintain clarity. At all costs, protect our children from VT. Childhood roots are the foundation for longevity. Hopefully, yours are deep and can withstand the storm. Your child's roots are growing. VT keeps them shallow and easily uprooted. Honor your warrior by protecting their legacy—our children. Review this checklist for helpful tips:

- Get training through a program like PsychArmor.
- Forgiving, but hold us accountable.
- Sexual rejection can be detrimental. Be responsible in this duty.
- Master the Five Love Languages.
- Attend church regularly.
- Get involved in your community.
- Refuse to rumor.
- Be adventurous.
- Stay positive.
- Help balance the ten life elements found in chapter 3.

Future Warriors

Some of the most resilient and well-rounded children I know have endured unimaginable things. People who come to terms with their disability are often happier than those who don't. Though military and first responder children may not suffer physical trauma, they are directly impacted by the hidden war their parent(s) fight. Millions of children across America, and billions around the world, have a parent serving in a job that may require the ultimate sacrifice at any given moment. This unstable life can torment their mind. They travel the world, are culturally diverse, and often experience much more than civilian children.

Military children can go months or years without a parent. They continue forward in life without their best friends, their mentors, their moms, or their dads. Stability is not a common theme in the military home.

Children of first responders have different challenges. Although their parents are ever-present, they face a community that is familiar with their parents' job. They may become targets of criminals that their parent arrested. They live in a state of hypervigilance. Each day these parents lose a little of themselves at work. This gradual shift after each traumatic event is different than what military kids experience. Trauma changes people. Being exposed to hostilities twenty-four-seven quickly alters a person's mentality. Children witness abrupt changes when their battle-hardened parents return home. This shift in emotion can cause dissension and insubordination. The ever-absent parent is heroic, while the ever-present parent may slowly lose respect through complacency.

To the sons and daughters of our warriors, please tune in. Your parents, whether they are in the military, law enforcement, fire-rescue, or another form of civil service, are part of a team that may require them to give their life. Maybe your parent died in the line of duty or was injured, your life may be an emotional roller coaster. It hurts and can feel unbearable at times. Your parent is a hero. They are symbols of hope and sacrifice willingly for humanity. They give you and I freedom from oppression, tyranny, and civil unrest. They do these things to provide us with the luxury of freedom and liberty. Remember to always be grateful for your soft bed, running water, house, vehicle, food, and much more. If you ever find yourself complacent in these things, I challenge you to go without.

You are an instrumental part of your family. Some parents are good at communicating gratitude, pride, and love. I cannot speak for those parents who are abusive or negligent. Only God can afford them mercy and grace. Forgiveness is your key to the door of sanctification. You cannot spiritually move forward in life without forgiving them, no matter the circumstance. Eventually, it'll be time for you to transfer to an A-Team of your own.

When you do, they will need the best you. Here are a few pointers to help you be a future warrior:

- Honor your parents.
- Respect authority.
- Carry your weight.
- Be obedient.
- Actively pursue a relationship.
- Do your best.
- Mirror your parent's good qualities and ignore the bad.
- Gracefully hold them accountable.
- Be merciful when they make mistakes.
- Love them unconditionally.

Guardian of the Warrior

Parents play a part in a warrior's rehabilitation. They are members of the team who can foster healing, stimulate good memories, and instigate post-traumatic growth. They are a reminder of the "good ol' days." But parents can also betray our fondest memories. Without even trying, they can sow seeds of discord. Spiteful chastisement, intentional manipulation, and a loose tongue are wrecking balls wrought for destruction. Parents must be as cunning as a serpent but as loving as a dove (Matthew 10:16).

Humility is a parent's greatest attribute. When warriors are in the storm, they need a lighthouse. Hidden Heroes and children are in the boat with their warrior, parents are not. They must be unwavering but willing to come to the rescue if necessary.

We read about a storm in the Bible that nearly drowned the disciples. That is, until they finally realized the impossibility of surviving without Jesus (Mark 4:38). Although they all woke Jesus up together, the idea of them perishing without Him originated from one person. On a warrior's A-Team, that responsibility rests with the parent. Parents cannot empathize like a friend and shouldn't sympathize like a spouse, but ought to muster courage and compassion to be wisely unbiased.

If you're a parent with a disabled warrior, your search for the most effective rehabilitation available, is over. First, let me applaud you for raising an American warrior - well done! But now it's time to rise up and revive hope.

Your first step is to pray. Your child was a gift from God, know that He is in ultimate control. This is your pathway to freedom from the burden of responsibility (Psalm 127:3). Acknowledge who they are now, not who they used to be. Your child needs you healthy and involved. Don't hesitate to send love their way every time you think of it. Here are a few tips that may help you help them:

- Love unconditionally.
- Believe in them.
- Limit your support (don't coddle, don't entitle, don't be their crutch).
- Be a listening ear (wait for them to solicit your advice).
- Be mindful of their experiences and their triggers.
- Acknowledge their value.
- Stay involved (invite them to family gatherings, visit, do things together).
- Never apologize for them.
- Show how proud you are of them.
- Get tuned in (don't make them explain everything).
- Know the name of their service dog and treat them like family.

Battle Buddy

The most authentic friends are difficult to find - a battle buddy who is loyal, thoughtful, and can anticipate a need before it arises. My oldest daughter was that friend for me. Our spiritual bond was unyielding. Verbal communication wasn't necessary; she just knew. Albeit time changes everything. For Jasmine, the time came for her to launch into adulthood. This left me with a significant void, which was soon filled.

Freddie C. Batista (aka Chino) came into my life via my little brother. Micah met Chino while attending the Huntmaster training course for the Youth Hunting Program of Florida. I felt an emptiness when my daughter left my team. Nobody could replace her, but could there be another who would measure up to my tactical expectations? The ability of foresight is an element of trust and spiritual connection. God sent Chino into my life at the right moment, but he too will eventually move on.

Friends should watch each other's back. Empathy is a connective emotion that stimulates mutual growth. Battle buddies who empathize are fellow warriors who have walked your mile. They don't give you a tissue; they give you a kick in the butt to revisit your *why*. Empathy is "Do it yourself," "Here's a straw," or "Rub some dirt on it." Insight is necessary for the resurrection of a warrior, but you only need one of these friends. If you have too many, you'll begin feeling beat down and unloved.

Sympathetic friends tend to coddle and enable. Like an empathetic friend, too many sympathizers can cause digression. Ultimately, we require a balance of friends and cohorts. Here's a list describing what friendships should look like:

- Communicate.
- Collaborate.
- Reciprocate.
- Defend each other.
- Work through problems.
- Respect and honor each other.
- Adventure life together.
- Sharpen one another.
- Anticipate each other's needs.
- Trust and be trustworthy.

Comrades

Be kind, respectful, diligent, and open-minded. Stay positive, even when things aren't comfortable. Many have never had the privilege of serving our country in uniform. Military and first-responder jargon are for warriors. Please don't use it carelessly or frown on us for speaking a language we understand.

A positive attribute of PTS is that it can liberate people from complacency, but it can be hazardous if not honed. We're neither black sheep nor part of the herd. Maintain your distance or announce your presence. Micromanagement is a no-go. Use condescending words like *"actually"*, *"okay"*, and *"listen"* sparingly. Be considerate in your actions and you'll get the best from us.

Respect our experiences and don't compare notes. Give credit where credit is due. Showing gratitude is more valuable than the verbal alternative. Allow us opportunities to succeed. Stay the course and do your job. Here's ten tips that may be helpful:

- Be a good listener.
- Avoid trying to "one up" with your own stories.
- Be compassionate by not hypersensitive.
- Be patient with our disability but discerning of our dependence.
- Offer meaningful help.
- Be genuine.
- Stay positive.
- Avoid pretending you understand if you don't.
- Stay in your lane and let us pass if we are going faster than you.
- Do your research before making assumptions. Don't be lazy.

Spiritual Leaders

Many spiritual leaders incur VC and STS. The continuous exposure to death, disease, and desperation takes its toll. Distant cousins to PTSD, VC and STS can be just as debilitating. However, it's important to point out that secondary exposure doesn't compare to firsthand experience.

Biblical knowledge offers sympathy, and that's good, but we often require empathy. Cognitive knowledge doesn't compare to experience. Most of you have never seen combat or had to engage a physical enemy. The idea that you comprehend our struggle is cause for objection. It's an honor to have stood on the front line for you, done your bidding, and taken one for the team. Most of us chose this path. We're not looking for superior treatment or constant gratitude, but we do want your respect and recognition that we, too, have a place in the Kingdom. Regardless of how many lives we've taken, the things we've destroyed, and the demons we carry, we bear the cross as well.

Trust and loyalty are traits that have become uncommon in Christianity. Some of the greatest skeptics I know are spiritual leaders. With all the conventional wisdom, biblical knowledge, and interpersonal skills, one would come to expect more vulnerability. Warriors without a cause need a compass. Tearing down barriers, overcoming transitional challenges, and connecting with like-minded individuals is key. Don't preach at us, but commune with us. Here are a few pointers that may draw more warriors to your church:

- Include, commune, and trust us.
- Abstain from self-righteousness but be righteous.
- Maintain Christ-like behavior; don't stoop to connect.
- Refrain from cultural biases and social standards.
- Pray with us, not for us.
- Work to overcome denominational segregation; collaborate with other ministries.
- Empower and use us for missions.
- Don't be afraid to speak conviction.
- Implement a specialized ministry for warriors - by warriors.
- Don't pretend; get someone who knows.
- Fight the podium effect.

Medical Personnel

The team wouldn't be complete without medical professionals who provide mental and physical care. To those who treat us like people and not numbers, thank you. You know us by name, and that's huge. You honor us by being prompt. You don't review our record right before our appointment. You are invested in our recovery.

Warriors, God gave these individuals special capabilities to navigate your psychological and physiological needs. They are vital in your resurrection, but don't blame them for your poor health if you're not doing your part. Physicians, psychologists, psychiatrists, and other specialists: the following ten tips are from a warrior survey that may help you be more impactful:

- Don't overbook appointments.
- Manage patient timelines.
- Treat us qualitative, not quantitative.
- Research our issues; don't just prescribe medications.
- Simplify healthcare.

- Listen with intent.
- Give us responsibility for our own health.
- Help us focus on the positive.
- Educate people with minor issues to stop overtaxing the system.
- Integrate spiritual wellness into the holistic concept.

The A-Team was a diverse group of individuals who came together for a just cause. They were the face of boldness, courage, and loyalty. There was no challenge too great, no schedule too full, and no need too deep that could keep them from completing their mission. Their impact on adolescents and emerging adults instilled a sense of defiance against tyranny. This show created heroic behavior tendencies in future warriors. For most, the A-Team was a symbol of hope in peril situations. Nearly everyone faces circumstances that feel hopeless. Each of us will one day embark on a journey of healing and restoration. Be artful in building a team around yourself.

Each member of your circle must be purposeful. Spiritual leaders, medical providers, comrades, battle buddies, and family members all play their part, but they must function synergistically. Putting others ahead of yourself and being willing to sacrifice in love and obedience delivers you from self-indulgent isolation. It prepares you to triumph in trials and tribulations. Service before self keeps you action oriented. Prayer is our greatest weapon from social enslavement and for peace of mind, but we must go beyond prayer.

God commanded us to be action driven. We shouldn't sit idly by waiting for God to do something, because He already did—He created you. He instilled talents in each of us to do our part. Some of us have skills in the great outdoors, some of us are athletes, some crunch numbers, some save lives, and some are philanthropists striving to shine a light in this dark world. When you look in the mirror and ask, "Why me?" answer, "Why not me?" You may be surprised by what you bring to the table. Each of us are divinely made and destined for greatness. Don't allow culture to define your happiness. Instead, live by your own terms inside the law. Maintain accord with your heavenly Father. Anything else is counterintuitive.

You can choose to be a liability or an asset. The free will that God gave you can often be the most challenging. Making ethical decisions in a society that promotes self-indulgence is difficult. It's like restraint at a buffet, keeping your eyes forward at the beach, or loving those who hate you.

Some parents raise children purposefully to become impact agents, and some parents disregard their duties altogether. In either case, the decision is yours and the judgment is God's. When you face overwhelming odds and find yourself surrounded by the enemy, you may want to consider letting out your battle cry.

Find your roar and hold your ground. Surrendering your life to Jesus allows you to fight through a losing battle. It sets you free from the dark shadows of worry. It unleashes the warrior inside and creates fear in your enemy. Your battle cry rallies your team, brings forth Jesus in your life, and rejuvenates the can-do attitude. While many of us feel like we face the world alone, the truth is that we all have someone in our corner. Whether it's someone in the literal sense or the spiritual, you are not alone.

3

THE CURE

The key to suicide prevention isn't in multimillion-dollar programs but in the core foundation of our will to survive. The great outdoors, a simplistic lifestyle, and a purpose-driven life are more important than the collage of bilateral pathways currently promoted. The truth of forgiveness and redemption is effective in saving heroes. Yet in our pursuit of intelligent thought, we have unnecessarily complicated the solution. This is not a one-size-fits-all approach. It is individually unique. I challenge you to test this antidote before objecting.

It is impossible to number humanity's past, present, and future. Among all humans who have ever existed, there's never been anyone quite like you. Nobody has ever owned your thumbprint. Trillions have existed, yet God knows you by name. The human mind can only comprehend so much. We can't count the stars, but we can grasp the concept of their design. The pattern of your thumbprint is the master plan for your destiny - your purpose.

Knowledge is power, but power can be disparaging when treated with derelict. Understanding the connection between physiology, psychology, and theology is vital in maintaining control of your command center—your mind. Your mind and body have mechanical inclinations that act as repeaters. In sports, they call this muscle memory. PTS becomes a spiritual infection when your experiences become you. However, owning your experiences is a survival tool. The difference is in perspective.

Spiritual infections can be influenced by chemical and nutritional composition. Uncontrollable cravings, sexual exploration, and violence are other examples of spiritual diseases affecting the physical realm. Spirituality alone may not be enough to save you, but you cannot receive the antidote without it.

In a recent study of the brain, neurotheologists provide evidence that believing in God activates the frontal lobe. "Engaging in spiritual practices raises levels of serotonin, which is the 'happiness' neurotransmitter, and endorphins" (Sandoiu, 2018). Many studies have discovered the healing power of spirituality, and nearly all research connects the brain to behavior. It's justifiable to claim that mental health and spiritual wellness interlock as one. Spirituality, however, seems to originate in the heart and not the mind. So how does one bridge the gap between the heart and mind?

Some Christian authors claim that there are eighteen inches between the heart and mind. A foot and a half separate us from freedom, victory, and abundant joy. Most of us are physically capable of taking an eighteen-inch step. But when it comes to spirituality, we get tripped up by worldly obstacles. We linger in doubt, personal interest, and scientific evidence. Bitter resentment, entitlement, and expectations deter us from taking this step forward. The enemy has booby-trapped our path and awaits in ambush. We require specialized training to identify and disarm devices of destruction, and this book is the manual for doing so. Steward Chase wrote, "For those who believe, no proof is necessary. For those who don't believe, no proof is possible."

Some individuals who suffer from mental health issues, like PTS, would argue that a cure is impossible. Many specialists also believe PTSD to be a lifelong burden. As one who struggled with PTSD for nearly five years, this denial was interrupted by enlightenment. Thousands of organizations have spent countless years searching for the best pathway to recovery, but this pursuit of calculable data can interfere with clarity. The cure is something one must discover individually.

A spiritual virus is like Stockholm syndrome. We adapt to our situation to survive, then grow convinced of its righteousness. It is quite challenging to rescue someone who doesn't want change. Convincing them that their capturer is bad is the first step in recovery. This revelation is the bridge to greener pastures. Take hold, and let's begin this journey from darkness to the light.

Many programs of rehabilitation are singularly focused and monetarily driven. Some religious leaders claim that faith alone is enough, but in my experience it's not. Medical practitioners put their trust in prescriptions, scholars in education, naturalists in nature, nutritionists in food, philanthropists in recreation, gardeners in soil, politicians in policies, and leaders in counseling. Yet suicides continue to happen at an alarming rate. Although each endeavor plays a vital part in the process of healing, the solution for curing PTSD and other mental health issues lies in a formula that holds an ingredient from each.

The key to overcoming PTS and stopping suicide is correctly balancing ten life elements. Live here in the now, not in yesterday or tomorrow. Believe you can, and you will. Know your worth. Identify the enemy. Push forward and live free.

"Attend today—succeed tomorrow" is a motto I heard at Webster Elementary School while mentoring students at career day in 2019. It epitomizes the premise of enduring yesterday and preparing for tomorrow by being grounded in the moment. Enjoy what you have, not what you lack. Free yourself from the enslavement of comparison.

It's okay to feel that the world is closing in around you! But know that this is an illusion, a tactic of the enemy to derail your purpose. A permanent solution to a temporary problem may drift across your mind, but don't feed it. Pain and sorrow can be overcome by taking those thoughts captive and throwing away the key. Complications and chaos, sleeplessness and nightmares, anger and rage can take a toll. Family and financial troubles can inflame destructiveness. Your fight, your journey, your war can be over, but don't go out in defeat. Don't kill yourself.

Why die in vain? Suicide is not an honorable death. It lacks courage and purpose. Do not be tricked by your mind to believe that your death will produce results. Hear my battle cry, ol warrior. Living is more productive than death by your own hand. In the storm, when your boat is sinking, wake Jesus.

Quitting now would mean that it was all for nothing. Your entire life, all your friends and family, and all your knowledge and experiences— gone. Your current troubles can be viewed as training to become a global impact agent. Those who struggle little - have little. Push forward and master the ability to balance life's most significant challenges.

This cure is both complex and straightforward. It's obtainable for those who believe. Some will suffer "paralysis from analysis" and get hung up on worldly influences. Although this cure is premanufactured inside each of us, many will never experience it. In the end, it is your responsibility to live your life, for the purpose you were designed for. Following are the ten life elements noted by warriors and affirmed by God:

- Personal Accountability
- Faith
- Family
- Friends
- Health
- Finances
- Purpose
- Nature
- Entertainment
- Rest

Each life element can be compartmentalized but must be balanced with the other nine. Holistic wellness is found when these elements are centered on God. Like ten spokes on a wheel, when one element is broken, then entire wheel is thrown off balance. Let's deep dive into each one.

Personal Accountability

For the best of us, we are our own worst enemy. We're hypercritical to perfect our purpose. In the name of convenience, progress, and success, we have filled our days with tireless efforts which drain our soul. We abuse our bodies and expect doctors to fix us. In an era of instant gratification, we consume medication like chickens scurrying around to fill their crops. We sue the pants off one another even when it's our fault. Although we suffer from iniquity, it's easier to identify other people's problems (Matthew 7:1–29). Deflection is a coping mechanism, but it creates a compilation of issues.

Thankfully, we have the cognitive capability to realize our fallacies and take corrective action. Although it may appear complicated to overanalytical individuals, this cure is quite simple. It must be accepted on layman terms and begins with taking responsibility for your life. Projecting your internal state onto others is a proponent of spiritual warfare. You either foster elements of love or embellish the destructiveness of hate. If it's the latter, then muster the courage to reform.

An aspect of personal accountability is navigating emotions. Move forward with precision and take responsibility for the footprints you leave behind. It is difficult to orient without a compass. Be it the high seas, open plains, or wild forests, the rules of north, east, south, and west cannot change by desire. Nor should the line between right and wrong be swayed by social influence. The Ten Commandments of the Bible are our moral compass. These ten rules of engagement provide direction for our life. Unlike the countless laws placed on us by our governments, these commandments are permissively beneficial. The government was ordained by God to serve and protect but has become self-serving.

Navigating the healing process begins internally. Blind people learn mobility without sight and often have better enlightenment than those who can see. Hidden wounds are obstacles within our consciousness. The commandments equip us to overcome these challenges. Let's look at how they shape personal accountability and produce healing.

- One God: Believing in only one God can be quite tricky. Many religious sects and denominational bouts are bidding for your soul. Making the right choice can be overwhelming. Pitches are persuasive, but so is the learned art of disbelief. Sometimes it may feel like it's easier to abstain from God altogether. Personal accountability isn't the absence of God but rather the influence by God. If you weigh the evidence, you'll discover that the facts point to a Trinity of one God. We are "created in His image," which comprises three parts: mind, body, and soul. We are either male or female, the way God intended. Free will allows us to choose right from wrong. Unguided decisions are stressful because the wrong choice can lead to everlasting damnation. The right decisions in life comes from moral conviction. God my Father is the figurehead, Jesus His Son and my lord is the admission ticket, and the Holy Spirit who connects us is the workhorse. You are a representative of yourself and the one you serve. You make things happen and are accountable for your actions. Christianity is a gift, just like your life. You can choose to own it or throw it away. Those in the "hurt locker" need hope, and a good dose of the Holy Spirit provides just that.

- Idols: When you close your eyes at night, what do you see? Is it hunting, family, sex, or...? A simple method of gauging idolatry is to do this once a day and see what owns your thoughts. The things that occupy your time the most may be an idol. Phone, work, pleasure, food, television, and family can, if not appropriately managed, ruin our relationship with God. The first commandment, to have only one God, is the most important because it determines the relationship we have with ourselves. Busyness deteriorates connectivity. Home in on spiritual matters and watch your purpose come to life.

- Blasphemy: Using God's name in vain is a form of blasphemy. Trendy and fashionable slang can seem innocent, but so can a little white lie. Telling someone "I'll pray for you" can be considered equally vile if you fail to follow through. Considering yourself godlike or behaving in such a way can qualify as blasphemy as well. Hypocrisy fits here too, as you misrepresent yourself and your creator. This section boils down to honor and respect. Do you honor God and respect yourself through actions and words?

- Sabbath: Our brains can handle sustained chaos for only so long. Six consecutive days of worldly influence and social pressure are exhausting. Anything more can be detrimental. A day of rest is prescribed by our heavenly doctor. Setting aside one day to do nothing (besides grow your relationship with God) gives your mind, body, and soul a chance to heal. It is crucial to be legalistic about this to ensure follow-through. Perusing social media, catching up, or chasing money without a day of rest will eventually lead to self-destruction. We use the sabbath to recharge. Allow yourself to regenerate and heal, clear your mind, and focus on God. At the end of the day, the only thing that matters is your accountability on judgment day. Many consider this a legalistic element of religion that no longer holds relevance. Some believe that Jesus set us free from this, but they would be wrong. He didn't come to abolish the law. God set this day aside for you because He cares about you individually.

- Honor Your Parents: The way we treat our parents is the way we'll treat our spouse one day. Parents don't always get it right, but neither do the children. To God, this is about your ability to reflect the mercy and grace He extends to you. How can we expect to receive something that we aren't willing to give? This grace isn't for them, after all. Honor, respect, and forgiveness are self-serving. They set you free from the bondage of judgement. Master this, and you'll discover a renewed sense of peace. Honoring your parents allows you joy and freedom from self-imprisonment. Heavenly honor is different than a worldly tribute, though. Human reputation is something we earn, whereas heavenly recognition is a gift. Jesus endured the worst humans could offer, and yet he still forgave them. Who are we to do otherwise?

- Murder: *Killing* and *murder* are synonymous in *Webster's Collegiate Dictionary 11th Edition* but flawed by humankind's interpretation. This commandment justifies arguments derived from personal agendas. The Bible is riddled with scripture that forsakes killing animals and people. However, the Bible also contains justifications to kill for protection and sustenance. It isn't the act but the reason that drives the action. Meat eaters who despise hunters are hypocrites. It is worse to loathe than to kill for food or protection. Killing out of anger, envy, or hurt is murder (this includes killing yourself). Killing for necessity is sanctified, but suicide will never be necessary because your circumstances can change if you take the eighteen-inch step toward salvation. Warriors who take the lives of bad people are justified if they take little pleasure in doing so. Whereas warriors who enjoy killing bad people have crossed a threshold of conviction. This behavior is often a coping mechanism, and when the killing ends, the struggle to return can feel impossible. Accidentally killing or murdering someone are forgivable offenses, but you must seek forgiveness. Confess and repent, then accept the gift of reconciliation. Being merciful to yourself is often the toughest part, though. True repentance comes from conviction, and conviction combats temptations.

- Adultery: Jesus said that inappropriate thoughts are the same as the act. I agree in spiritual terms but feel it necessary to provide clarity for personal responsibility. Jesus is teaching us here that we can control our actions by controlling our thoughts. Not to sound contradictory to Jesus but thinking it and doing it are on different levels. Fluttering thoughts fill our minds with sex, rage, legacy, hate, envy, greed, pride, trauma, and suicide, often without provocation. These thoughts are not what Jesus was talking about; rather He refers to grabbing hold of a provocative idea and fantasizing about it. The power of your mind regulates your existence and your actions. You can starve the wolf of fornication by ignoring temptations and controlling your environment. The fleshly pleasure obtained through adultery can be found elsewhere. If you need to satisfy this craving, get creative with your mate. Temptation becomes sin when we act it out in our minds, which eventually leads to doing it in the flesh. Control your thoughts and you'll find victory.

- Stealing: This most often occurs from a sense of entitlement. Although, some people steal out of necessity. I do not believe there is a separation of morality here. Anything you take should be returned in time, talent, or treasure - give it back however you can. Thieves are repulsive, cowardly, and lack restraint. Stealing is disrespectful to God, yourself, and others. A society of instant gratification breeds thieves because people don't want to work for things. Learn patience and overcome this lure. Seek forgiveness from God and repay the debt. You may find yourself with a broken nose or worse if you seek forgiveness from the person you stole from, but if that's how you feel led, then go for it. Overcoming the urge to steal can be done through the "earn it" mentality.

- Lying: Telling the truth takes courage and reflects morality. This commandment is connected to every other commandment. Lying is a seedling of immorality. We have grown accustomed to "good lies" and "bad lies," but the fact of the matter is that they're both manipulations of information. Each of us must discern the true nature of our intentions, but I don't believe God will justify a lie. However, electing to withhold information for a just cause may be ok. There is a thin line between lying and divulging the truth. Transparency can be fruitful, but it can also be destructive. The pursuit of righteousness eliminates the need to lie. Lying handcuffs spirituality.

- Covet: Desiring what other people have creates displeasure, but it can also be a motivational tool. Discontentment fractures the foundation of morality. We are in this place, at this moment, and have the things around us for a reason. Mark Twain and President Theodore Roosevelt noted that "comparison is the thief of joy". Coveting creates a disgruntled attitude that may lead to a violation of other commandments. Those with great possessions are often poor in spirit. Less is often more. The measure of success isn't in property but in happiness. Be content with what you have and who you are, but don't let this be an excuse for laziness. Personal responsibility should instigate a desire for self-efficacy. Maintain a balanced lifestyle and remain satisfied but work hard to earn your keep. Dream big but be realistic, because reaching for the stars put us on the moon.

The first four commandments focus on our relationship with God, the Creator. The next five focus on our relationships with other people (the peace that passes understanding, love others, starve the evil wolf, want something, work for it, and be honest). The very last commandment is for us as individuals. Although they are in order of priority, I have found it helpful to go in reverse order. Laying the foundation of personal accountability provides sustenance for you to build a house of self-improvement. You must first believe in yourself before you can have faith in someone else.

Faith

Trust, loyalty, hope, and commitment are the cornerstones of faith. Everyone has faith, but not everyone puts their faith in the right noun. This misguidance causes disappointment, hurt, and pain. Some people claim that belief in God also produces distress, and they are right. Disenchantment occurs when expectations go unmet. We often place unachievable expectations on ourselves, family, friends, medicine, products, and even on God (not that God has limitations).

We struggle to balance natural with supernatural. This limitation is due to cognitive limitations. Religion assembles people under theological comprehension. Denominations create segregation within a religion that fosters alternatives. The variances among religions are what followers believe. For Christians, it is freedom in Jesus. This salvation is a choice and an entitlement. Complications exist when people think they're Christian but produce the fruit of this world or no fruit at all (Matthew 7:15–20). It's a gift under the Christmas tree with your name on it. Will you open it?

Surrender or fight is the question that often separates heroes from cowards. But what about surrender *to* fight? It may appear at first to be an oxymoron, but it's not. *Surrendering* is not synonymous with *quitting*. These contain two different characteristics. When someone quits, they give up. Quitters (unless they quit something like smoking, porn, stealing, lying, cheating, etc.) often have little skin in the game. They value little and are quick to tap out when things get tough. Suicide can be a product of this. Surrendering, on the other hand, is signified by an individual who was willing to give it all but sees reason in playing the long game.

To surrender is to get a hard reset, an opportunity to redesign your battle plan. To quit is to stop fighting altogether. The hidden war we face requires spiritual combat training. This training fortifies your defenses. Few warriors go into battle without proper training. Doing so will get you killed. It's time to organize a counterattack with high power support.

Military personnel go behind enemy lines believing their government has their back. We have faith in this higher power, often without ever meeting our Commander in Chief. It's important to grasp this point. We commit to the government without meeting them in person but often feign trusting a supernatural power. Our government knows little about you, but God knows you intimately. The government asks you to die for them, but Jesus willingly laid down his life for you. This comparison is an appeal to accept Christ as your Lord and Savior. If you hunger for positive change, to live life abundantly with unspeakable peace, then you're on the right page. You must surrender your soul to God to spiritually fight back.

Having faith is simple. Determining what you should believe is where most spiritual disagreements occur. Faith isn't religious; rather, religion originates from faith. However, religious sects can deviate from the origin of faith. Loyalty to a church (lowercase C) is the apparatus for segregation. Instead, one should commit to the Church (capital C). We are, after all, interchangeable. Instead of focusing on church development (worldly power), we should concentrate on Church growth (heavenly power). Recruiting you into the Kingdom as the warrior you are is my dream. Watching you be swallowed up by the world is my nightmare. You are an asset to the King, an invaluable impact agent, a crusader. Take the leap of faith and transform your moral wounds into spiritual artillery.

Many of you receive tactical training. You learn methods to defeat an opposing force. Few, however, receive training to Survive, Evade, Resist, and Escape (SERE). There are usually two options when faced with an overwhelming enemy force. The combat code is to surrender only if the means justify the ends. In other words, surrender if you can no longer cause harm to the enemy. If captured, combat personnel are authorized to give brief information. Those who are captured survive because they keep hope alive. Knowing that a mighty force is planning your rescue fortifies your spirit to live on.

Unequivocally, there are always two forces at play: good and evil. The superior power (good) will win, you must be on the right side to taste victory. Christianity is the perfect way of life if we can overcome the human condition. Warriors become disgruntled when they discover corrupt deeds behind the "just" war. Real Christianity is absent of politics, greed, corruption, scandals, hate, envy, lust, addictions, temptations, competition, racism, sexism, and the lot. It is the perfect solution for the embattled soul. Instead of quitting, try surrendering.

Learning the art of spiritual warfare requires us to consider previous training null and void. Surrendering in battle is frowned upon but essential in faith. Courageous acts amid imminent defeat define our country's heroes. Deep within our souls lies a warrior's ethos, a hero, ready and willing to fight to the death. But death in the flesh means life in the spirit. It's time to retrain for the battle ahead. Quitting is not a viable option; surrendering is. I want to commission you as an impact agent for God – a warrior for the Kingdom. If you're ready to surrender for a chance to fight back, then stop what you're doing, find a quiet place, and pray these words:

God…hear my battle cry. I've fought and resisted, stood my ground, and carried these burdens far too long. I confess my sins and surrender my life to you. I accept your Son as my Savior, the Holy Spirit as my guide, and you as my Commander. I'm yours for reinvention. Forgive me, Father, and help me abstain from fleshly desires. Fill me with love and soften my hardened heart. Restore my brokenness. Grant me patience, the courage to live faithfully, and the ability to hear your call. I want to be a light and will follow biblical guidance. Wash, purge, and renew me. You gave your only Son for me. He died on the cross to free me from the burden of righteousness. He defeated death and is alive today. I, too, wish to die a worthy death, but first, allow me to live a purposeful life. I'm ready for rescue. Accept me and free me, Lord. Amen.

CONGRATULATIONS and welcome to the team. Claiming that prayer as your own unloads your overweight pack. You are hereby released from prison and pardoned from all your sins. I'm extremely excited to call you brother or sister and look forward to serving with you. You're now part of an eternal community that is more spectacular than anything you can imagine. You are free from spiritual hunger and thirst, greed and corruption, lies and manipulation, insecurities and fear, death and destruction. You now have lasting purpose and meaning. God is rejoicing, and heaven is throwing a party just for you. Imagine that—the Creator of everything is celebrating you. There is healing for your moral wounds, relaxation from hypervigilance, and relief from the burdens weighing you down. You are free to live without the fear of death, free from obsoletion, free from evil. You are free indeed!

Now that you're spiritually fit to fight, we claim triumph over self-destruction. You have fatally wounded suicidal thoughts. In the name of Jesus, the seed to your cure has sprouted. Faith is the core of your wholeness, but you must cultivate it, or weeds will overtake it. You must nurture it, or it will wilt and perish. You must be the farmer of your own health and wellness. At the end of the day, standing at the pearly gates of heaven on judgment day, it'll be just you and God. Push forward through this book to finish learning about spiritual combat training.

Every human in the world is born with a moral compass. This divine phenomenon connects humanity. Every culture across the globe is convicted by the Ten Commandments and have laws that reflect such. All religions point to a higher power, but knowing Jesus sets us free from theological complications.

Practicing a religion is the act of doing something repeatedly based on obligation, whereas faith creates actions based on desire. Faith is the proponent of being good to go, no matter how broken you are. It is the essence of something hoped for, while religion provides a structured outline to aid in our daily walk. Religious obligations complement faith, but please don't misunderstand—they can mislead as well. It's easier to be part of the Church if you're a member of a church in your community. Although the Church is the singular body of Christ, churches are members of the body.

It's important to note that flawed humans lead each church. Most do their best to revere God, so let's cut them some slack. Understanding this may help lower your expectations for the perfect pastor and will keep you plugged in. Find a church that fits your life experiences and your purpose.

As a Christian, I yearn to do good works, even though there's no obligation. Love fuels this conviction. In the book *The Five Love Languages*, Gary Chapman depicts five ways for us to communicate our love more effectively for one another. Chapman helps us understand and navigate a silent language, saving many relationships. This book captures an expression of the Holy Spirit. No matter what culture you live in, it applies to all. By understanding the five love languages, we can enhance our relationship with God. In so doing, we'll gain a desire to serve. Going to church feeds our soul, but if all you do is eat, you'll get fat and lazy. On the other hand, if you don't eat, you'll starve.

Now that we've laid the foundation for your home, it's time to add the next life element. Remember, this book is a step-by-step process designed to get you back up to speed. If you move forward without getting right with God, then you'll be spinning your wheels. Everything from this point on will be in vain. Building a house without first laying the foundation reflects a lack of love and self-efficacy. For the sake of your family, build your house on solid ground.

Family

Healing happens at home, but so does hurtfulness. Family is the cornerstone of rehabilitation and the fortification of your legacy. They allow reinvention and exploration of new norms. Spouses pick you up when you're down, clean your messes (related to your disability, not laziness), and provide pleasure. This synergy goes both ways, though. One should not expect to receive without giving. Otherwise, you'll become like the Dead Sea - always getting but never giving. You can build your house around family and still feel homeless. Give and cultivate love daily.

Military spouses sacrifice greatly and wear many hats. They take command of the household when their warrior deploys but then forfeits authority upon their return. They are masters of flexibility, endurance, and selflessness. For warriors who return home wounded, these Hidden Heroes transform into medical caregivers, psychologists, booking agents, timekeepers, coaches, and cheerleaders. They work relentlessly to maintain peace in and out of the home. In most cases, warriors should not share their demons with family. Doing so has resulted in countless broken marriages. Sharing traumatic experiences with someone spiritually connected to you could result in vicarious trauma. Instead, lean on professionals or trusted friends.

Law enforcement and fire-rescue spouses are spectacular in their own way. They do not sacrifice as military spouses do, but their role in our communities is just as significant. They too are the Hidden Heroes behind the scenes, keeping their warriors motivated and driven to serve hometown communities. These unsung heroes must remain vigilant against hostile encounters, health issues, and spiritual infections. They are on the frontline of our battlefield. Our courage is fueled by our love for them and their love for us.

Take your war with demonic forces far away from your family. Expelling evil spirits in the wild keeps them from infiltrating others, but be careful not to fight alone. We cannot cast out our own demons. Jesus spent forty days in the wilderness fortifying His resilience, but He had a team. His spiritual connectivity to the Father was rock solid. Jesus prevailed by focusing on His purpose, not superficial glory. Find your purpose, and you may discover a path to revival.

It's better to suffer forty days in the wilderness than a lifetime in misery. However, do not attempt a forty-day wilderness purge without proper training. Death may occur, but so might life. You accept all risks. Your life is your responsibility. The decisions you make requires an eighteen-inch step forward. Nobody will come until you call for rescue.

Two of life's most significant priorities are all too often taken for granted. Faith and family are nearly always on the mind when death closes in, but in life we tend to be careless with them. Almost everyone worries about what's coming next, while those who are close to God welcome the transition. The most common regret expressed by people who are about to die is that they wish they had done more with their family. Be wise and reprioritize life now to alleviate this sorrow later.

The greatest parenting advice I ever received was a gift from my child: "A hundred years from now, it will not matter what my bank account was, the sort of house I lived in, or the kind of car I drove, but the world may be different because I was important in the life of a child." I will keep this gift forever. It is a grounding point that reminds me of what I'm doing right.

Family is an intangible gift that provides meaning. It gives warriors a reason to fight, to die, and—often more difficult—to live. All of us are products of human reproduction, but not everyone receives the gift of family. This emptiness is due in part to a misunderstanding of what family comprises. It isn't a bloodline, rather a spiritual bond. Legacies emerge when bloodline and spiritual bonds connect. Family can disappoint, but they can also set the bar for extraordinary acts of bravery. Learn from both and take steps toward restoring your family.

Becoming a parent is one of the toughest yet most rewarding things you'll ever do. It's important for parents to realize our differences. When people claim to be a parental expert because their child is perfect, recognize that God saw their inability to handle a challenging child. Consistent parenting that results in different outcomes may cause parents to wonder where they went wrong. The world will cast judgment and claim that a lousy child is the product of poor parenting. Poor parenting may be the case in some situations, but not all. If you struggle with a difficult child but you're a good parent, then know that you're not alone. Lean on Proverbs 22:6 and set the example of resilience, grace, mercy, and love. Your child is learning character traits from your response to their misdealing's. It's okay to get it wrong from time to time. Although parenting is the number-one job that shapes our world, it's important to release yourself from the burden of righteousness. Otherwise, making a mistake could lead to your self-destruction. Everyone, even your children, is on an individual journey in life. Warriors would rather take fire from an enemy force than watch their children go down the wrong road. When the devil can't get to you, he'll go after your children.

Suicidal ideations often arise from family misconduct. At that moment when the storm is raging, you may feel that there's no way out. Imagine the peril of being in the Bahamas in September of 2019 when Hurricane Dorian raged overhead for nearly seventy-two hours. Chaos and mass destruction are occurring all around you, but you hold on for dear life. It's easy to fight for survival when it's an outside force but grim when it's internal.

Externalizing internal battles is a critical step in spiritual warfare. Suicide is often a coward's way out, whereas pushing forward is heroic. It's what warriors do to overcome an enemy force. Taking ground from the enemy is more rewarding than giving it up. Time proves that all things come to pass. Remember, suicide is a permanent solution to a temporary problem. There is always a choice. Muster the grit to hold on and avoid making a catastrophic, family-altering decision that creates more problems than solutions. Brick for brick, the foundation you have with family is much stronger than the torment you suffer. Warrior up and fight on!

Friends

Defined by actionable extent, friends are people who listen, lend a hand, mentor, and jump into the foxhole with you. My five pillars of friendship are: trust, loyalty, accessibility, communication, and kinship. All too often we misinterpret friendliness for friendship. Friendly people give empty promises, whereas friends follow through. Remember, though, they too have lives to live. Fellowshipping with friends is an integral part of the healing process. The camaraderie with like-minded individuals is irreplaceable. However, be prepared to be alone. Like the framework of your home, friends aren't always visible. But if you knock on the walls, you'll discover that they're all around you.

We share information with close friends and hope it stays confidential. This connectivity allows us to release negative energy before navigating forward. A warrior's circle should mirror the twelve disciples. Jesus chose friends from all walks of life with unique experiences, but they all had one thing in common. Of the twelve, few were on the inside. Although Jesus maintained a small circle of friends, He was friendly with everyone on the outside. Being kind doesn't mean ignoring deviant behavior. In fact, it requires corrective action through peaceful mediation. Unfortunately, our culture has lost the art of friendly interaction outside our circles.

Fame and greed are two detrimental interests that corrupt our spirit. The desire for power is bad if it's linked to fame or greed. A positive person with authority can be a productive impact agent. These influential individuals reshape cultures. Identical friends create redundancies. The wrong kind of friends will have adverse consequences. With too many friends, you'll become overwhelmed with obligations. Friendship requires precision and reciprocation. The group dynamic must be fluent, or it will self-destruct.

Friendship is different than friendliness. How is it possible to treat repulsive individuals kindly? In a way, it's quite simple; but on the other hand, it's tough. Many of us have pet peeves and triggers that anger us. Someone being inconsiderate, rude, spiteful, shady, manipulative, or hostile can ignite rage. However, there are de-escalation techniques that provide spiritual self-aid and buddy care. The world knows this as humility, but for Christians it is grace and mercy.

Bless those who curse you, love those who hate you, be gentle to the wicked and firm to the righteous. Applaud those who cheat you, support those who deny you, and ignore wrongful accusations. It's okay to defend yourself but do so in love. Kindness is not weakness, and silence is not ignorance. The truth is revealed in time. Decompressing is a vital step in emotional sustainability. You must have a friend who will draw fire, someone who has your back and allows you to vent without judgment or know-it-all feedback. An empathetic friend will adventure with you without saying a word. They know your pain and suffering and will refute self-pity. Without friends supporting your eighteen-inch step, you cannot advance to the next life element. Physical and mental health are interconnected. One cannot be without the other, but only one will condemn your soul to hell.

Health

Your overall health and wellness begin with personal accountability. We depict food industries as evil, welfare as crippling, and doctors as uncaring, but these are murmurs of cultural implosion. It reflects irresponsible behavior. We have given control of sustenance to organizations instead of relying on ourselves. Most Americans depend on grocery stores to survive. The convenience factor, along with busyness, deters most people from growing their own food.

Many people are born into poverty. Welfare has become an entitlement instead of emergency aid. Research has discovered that chemical imbalance, due to unhealthy food, is a leading cause in genealogical poverty. We starve our bodies from nutritional balance, consume foods that are quick and easy, then expect doctors to magically fix us. This equation is all wrong. Obtaining good health is not complex at all, and there is a simple solution that anyone can obtain.

The health of your internal organs is essential to feeling good. Gut flora, for example, is central to your body's functionality. It would be appropriate to consider health as the amenities of your home. Appliances, plumbing, and electricity are luxuries we often take for granted. Likewise, many of us take our health for granted. Using an outhouse, burning candles, and braving the elements can realign perspective and foster an appreciation for simple pleasures. Maybe that's how we should look at food!

A multitude of studies provides evidence that fitness is a leading factor in health and wellness. Dr. Alfredo Morabia and Dr. Michael C. Costanza (2004) found that walking thirty minutes a day enhances vitality, thus increasing life span. Folkins, Carlyle, Sime, and Wesley (1981) discovered that physical fitness improves people's happiness and reduces stress. Lanza, Short, et al. (2008) teamed up to prove exercise as a critical component of longevity and productivity. If these references aren't enough to convert you into a fitness guru, then consider the findings of De Moor, Beem, et al. (2006). They reported in their paper "Regular Exercise, Anxiety, Depression, and Personality: A Population-Based Study": "Regular exercise is cross-sectionally associated with lower neuroticism, anxiety and depression and higher extraversion and sensation." According to ScienceDirect, "Extraversion is a broad personality trait that encompasses a number of more specific characteristics such as sociability, assertiveness, high activity level, positive emotions, and impulsivity," whereas "neuroticism is a broad personality trait that reflects the extent to which a person experiences the world as stressful, threatening, and problematic." According to Sigmund Freud (1856–1939), many who suffer neuroticism can link this pessimistic mindset to their childhoods.

Suffering from chronic pain or a disability can hinder engagement in traditional forms of exercise. Refusing or limiting physical activity for fear of making it worse can lead to a digression in health. This reservation can lead to poor mental health, which often capitulates chronic pain. Healthcare providers are finally recognizing and treating the connection between mental health and physical pain. There are abundant resources on adaptive forms of exercise, but you must be willing to cross your psychological limitations.

Take on a forty-day "Warrior Up" challenge and become victorious in the battle for your life. Remember to take necessary safety precautions to avoid injury or death. This hard reset is imperative to regain balance in your life and is a critical step to combat suicide. You don't have to be at your wits' end to fight back though.

There are exercise routines for everyone. Your abilities will dictate what you can do physically. Balancing input with output is essential in managing a fit-to-fight model. *Fit to fight* depicts our readiness for any situation at any time. It encompasses the mind, body, and soul. A warrior's job is to remain combat ready. Being wounded or injured does not excuse a warrior from the obligation to fight. Though your organization may no longer require your services, you still have a responsibility to yourself, your family, and your community.

At any given moment, you may be called upon to dawn your "battle rattle." It may be an internal or external attack, so remain physically and spiritually ready. A war is at your front door. Your life, up to this moment, has been training to prepare for this battle. Are you ready for war?

A lethargic attitude, complacency, and misplaced priorities are three showstoppers. Disabilities are often excuses bound in entitlement. It's important to remember that we earned our stripes as warriors, and now must earn our life daily. These scars are an honor and privilege to wear. They remind us of our service and sacrifices. Let the pain that inflicts you physically be the driving force that motivates you spiritually. Confront the laziness that drives failure. Focus on the type of fuel you put into your system and throttle up. Gear your exercise to match your capabilities. Execute.

Do you live to eat or eat to live? Food equals vitality—it is an essential life element. We cannot go without food for sustained periods. It's like taking flight in an aircraft without refueling first; when you're empty, you crash. For the sake of brevity, I've lumped food and hydration together under this life element. Consume too much, and gluttony occurs. Consume too little, and we wither away. Our minds and bodies (and souls) produce results from our intake. Attitude and energy are the output from our input.

Survivalists know that the body can sustain itself on energy reserves for three weeks without food and three days without water. This is only possible if output is minimalized. High-performance vehicles require high-performance fuel; otherwise, they won't produce the desired results. The same goes for you. If you're in a high-demand, high-stress environment, then you need a high-performance diet. Eat and drink with a purpose.

Years of research, development, and personal experimentation led to the discovery of homeostasis, which is the body's ability to heal itself given the right balance of vitamins and nutrients (real foods). Supporting these findings is Dr. William W. Li, a world-renowned physician, scientist, speaker, and author of *Eat to Beat Disease: The New Science of How Your Body Can Heal Itself*. *Homeostasis* is defined as "the tendency toward a relatively stable equilibrium between interdependent elements, especially as maintained by physiological processes." The theory of homeostasis supports the Warrior Up challenge. Everyone who accepts this test undergoes a transformation. Dropping all meat and wheat products for forty days may provide a newfound sense of health and wellness. This "Warrior Diet" requires discipline and endurance. If strictly followed, you should be able to get back into the fight and find freedom from slavery to pharmaceuticals. Note, however, that this is a lifestyle change. After the forty-day fast, you should maintain this diet throughout the week, incorporate organic meat (like wild game) on weekends, remove processed sugar, and foster a purposeful lifestyle.

Many churches refer to a similar diet as the Daniel's Fast, but don't get confused. This focuses on Daniel 10:1–21 as a three-week program for spiritual growth, whereas the Warrior Diet reflects on Daniel 1:8–14 for optimal holistic results. The Bible tells the story of Daniel and his friends outperforming their peers after consuming just vegetables and water for ten days. Daniel's Fast was investigated in 2010 by Lipids Health and Disease, who concluded that the twenty-one days of modified dietary intake that the fast recommends is 1) well tolerated by men and women and 2) reduces several risk factors for metabolic and cardiovascular disease (Bloomer, Kabir, et al., 2010). Personal accountability is a cornerstone for healing. It's evident that an indiscreet diet may be a leading factor in your poor mental and physical health.

A thorough investigation of the Bible leads to understanding God's divine hand on sustenance. No other book provides real-life advice as comprehensive and fruitful as the Holy Word. You'll find guidance on nearly every life situation, including superior diets. You should do your research, though. A quick and convenient method is using an online search tool. For brevity, let's look at a few well-known references.

The book of Leviticus offers a legalistic perspective of dietary restrictions that guided the Israelites during unsanitary times (Leviticus 11:1–47). Jesus, however, debunked this religious restriction by declaring all things good to eat (Mark 7:17–19). We should take caution in our interpretation of this, however, as Jesus was depicting that which defiles the soul. He wasn't necessarily relieving us of the burden of health-conscious decisions. Some vegetarians and vegans reference the book of Leviticus as their beacon, while Seventh-Day Adventists employ it as a religious measure for obedience and devotion. Biblical perspective empowers us with freedom of choice, not to be mistaken for convenience. In 1 Corinthians 6:19–20, we are directed to care for our bodies because we are vessels for God, a temple of the Holy Spirit.

Lazy consumers attack denominational theology to justify convenience. Both medical research and biblical evidence support the theory that a poor diet leads to poor health. Personal accountability deters you from this destructive path. The US Food and Drug Administration enacts strict protocols for safety, but digestible food isn't the same as healthy food. Processed sugar, for example, is unnatural and unhealthy. Consuming sugar-filled products and other processed foods reduces your body's ability to fight. In 2015, Ullah, Akhtar, and Hussain researched "Effects of Sugar, Salt and Distilled Water on White Blood Cells and Platelet Cells." Their discovery aligns with countless others in the field of health and wellness. They found that sugar reduces white blood cell count by 40 percent. White blood cells are essential for your body to defend itself and to obtain homeostasis. Consuming sugar is like adding sand to your vehicle's gas tank. In a highly volatile situation, when you need your vehicle to accelerate quickly, you may find yourself jammed up. Mediocre food equals poor health, which leads to chronic pain, bad attitudes, and ultimately self-destruction.

The concept of the Warrior Diet is simple: eat to live to fight to win. Whether you're fighting a hidden battle or a sanctioned war, the food you consume will determine your ability to perform. The medical community is primarily reactive and reap the rewards from your poor health. Billions of dollars are relying on you to continue making bad dietary choices. The corporate departments are counting on you. However, you have the power to disappoint. Take back your life and stop being a slave to the system. For veterans, the Veterans Administration (VA) orders us to consume medications. Failure to do so could result in loss of entitlements. Warriors who are not self-reliant often become enslaved to the medical system. Healthcare providers can be as hurtful as they are helpful if not balanced with autonomous care.

To overcome this obstacle, you must take a leap of faith and replace your desires with needs – eat purposefully. Within the first week of the Warrior Diet, I was able to drop all prescribed medications. There was a noticeable change in mood, clarity of mind, and peace. My stamina began to return. Although a fractured cervical spine and other physical impairments remained restrictive, the chronic pain associated with these injuries significantly reduced. My PTS started to abate, and I gained control over provocative thoughts. The forty-day purge was grueling, but the reward exceeded it beyond measure.

The Bible may appear conflicting at times, but in its entirety, it is quite conclusive. Eat things in season, harvest and consume wild game, and grow a garden. If you look closely and understand the full content of God's Word, you'll discover that it's okay to consume all good things in moderation. Our bodies are uniquely designed vessels, and it's our responsibility to understand it individually. While we're all created equal in spirit, we're physically unique.

It may appear in the previous paragraphs that I think medical professionals are problematic. If this was your conclusion, then you've misunderstood. Medical professionals save lives, but they should not be held liable for your health. That's your job! This is a deflection that many reckless individuals suffer - always blaming others. Health and wellness are a personal responsibility, just like salvation. Most people who join the medical community do so to help others. Unfortunately, we cannot help people who don't help themselves. As the saying goes, "You can lead a horse to water, but you can't make it drink."

Although homeostasis is sovereign health care, we must capitulate to medical treatment because it is a crucial part of holistic wellness. Some health-related issues cannot resolve through self-care. The medical community is absolutely, unconditionally necessary. They provide therapies, pharmaceuticals, surgery, research and development, education, and awareness, and they save countless lives daily. They are invaluable to our communities. If you have a medical concern, you should see a specialist. Do not, however, get angry or impatient with them. They are working in an overloaded system, trying to keep up with careless or uneducated people. When we accept the terms of ownership for our health and wellness, we convert from entitled to empowered.

Finances

Some of us work to live, while others live to work. The Bible says that the love of money is the root of all evil, not money itself (1 Timothy 6:10). If you spend more time thinking about money than anything else, then you live to work. This puts you on the edge of greed, a soul-eating machine that will consume your life. Chasing money won't bring you happiness. Countless millionaires and famous people have committed suicide because they sought fulfillment in worldly pleasures. Aspiring for financial prosperity isn't wrong but caution yourself to ensure that it doesn't become more than a tenth of your lifestyle. Stability and success are often confused with earned income, but status means nothing to God.

Everyone is in pursuit of the same thing. Unless you trust God with your finances, you'll never experience lasting joy.

The worldly lie that happiness is for sale is misleading. Some pursue power for gratification, while others seek freedom from restrictions. Some people work to give their families a better way of life, while others work to survive poverty. According to Catherine Rampell (2009), "Of all the common things couples fight about, money disputes were the best harbingers of divorce. For wives, disagreements over finances and sex were good predictors of divorce, but financial disputes were much stronger predictors. For husbands, financial disagreements were the only type of common disagreement that predicted whether they would get a divorce." Thus, finances are considered the leading cause of divorce in America. While minimal data exists to claim that financial hardship is a leading cause of suicide, it's easy to connect the dots to show that financial instability causes enough strife to destroy families. The value of family to warriors predicates the self-destructive behavior that stems from economic insecurity. It's like having a house with no roof. How can you protect your home without cover?

Imagine being responsible for national defense. You are the one person who stands between freedom and oppression. You were wounded during a terrorist attack and were subsequently relieved of duty. You're now home with your family, and your disability check is barely keeping your bills paid. The VA sends a letter threatening to reduce your rating, which will subsequently lead to homelessness for you and your family. It's because of your military service and moving your family from place to place that your wife restarted her career countless times. Her income is barely enough to provide food. Your refusal of unproductive treatment may very well cost you your benefits. Your decision not to play the game has jeopardized your home, and now you question your value to your family.

Are you an asset or a liability? How can someone with so much to offer become so insignificant? The monster begins to emerge. Thoughts start to seep in that your family is better off without you. You have the means to remove the threat to your family and begin to calculate the pros and cons. You desire a fruitful death, but you're not willing to destroy the thing you love the most. The pressure begins to boil your blood. You reach out for help but find a self-serving bureaucratic system. You reach for your gun, chamber a round, and press the cold steel against your temple. Your gut churns, and you feel both heavy and empty. A mix of anger, frustration, denial, then guilt overcomes you. You recount that God has a purpose for your life, but when is that supposed to happen?

The words "Surrender, but don't quit," "Stay in the fight," and "Daddy, I love you" echo through your mind. You realize that finances should be only a tenth of your life, but you've given it more. You recognize the imbalance and decide to put the gun down. A flood of emotions overwhelms you, and you cry out to God, but there's no answer. How can your Father be catatonic at this moment? The silence is deafening, but you remember that this conflict is your spiritual war. You've taken fire before and have fought back bravely. The only difference now is that you're in hand-to-hand combat with a hidden enemy that's infiltrated your command center. Financial stability will continually be an issue because others will always be a factor. Don't allow this section greater influence than the other nine. It is equal to all others and must remain centered on God. Keep guard because this is an extremely effective weapon for the enemy.

Purpose

Someone who loses their purpose can often feel useless. One of the greatest difficulties for military personnel transitioning into civilian life is redefining their sense of purpose. This is similar for first responders retiring from service. They go from living a lifestyle of trust, camaraderie, belonging, and life-saving missions to being a number lost in a world of untrustworthy, fake, and petty civilians. This transition can devastate people of valor. That moment when you take off your boots, hang up the uniforms, and realize a diminished significance. We now have our freedom and worldly pleasures, but we've lost our purpose (or so we think).

A man or woman without a purpose is like a ship deprived of its captain, drifting in the ocean with no destination. When a storm approaches, chaos ensues, and the ship begins to sink. A warrior without a purpose is like a church without parishioners. Give us something to fight for so we don't battle ourselves. However, we don't have to look far to discover that our lives outside the uniform still has meaning. For many, our greatest fear is a fruitless death. Being in or out of uniform doesn't change that.

The Dong Ap Bia mountain in Vietnam, also known as Hamburger Hill, is a perfect illustration. Hundreds of soldiers lost their lives to take that mountain, all just to hand it back to the enemy a little while later. Law enforcement officers experience similar situations in uniform when perpetrators are quickly released. Uniforms don't dictate purpose; people do.

Your perspective and self-worth are the main factors in a purpose-driven life. Race, gender, religion, class, and status play no part in your purpose. However, society and culture do. You can have the answer to world peace, the cure for cancer, or the formula for perfect parenting, but if it lacks acceptance, then you fail. Rejection fosters resentment, which breeds internal conflict. You do not have to create something from scratch to have purpose and fulfillment. It is an illusion to believe leadership a proponent of legacy and worth. If you genuinely want to make a difference, fight for something more than yourself.

Although purpose is only a tenth of a well-balanced life, it is part of the entire circle. Every life element benefits your purpose. Pastor Rick Warren captures the essence of a fruitful spirit in his book *Purpose Driven Life* (2002). Such a spirit enhances faith, unifies family, forms friendships, focuses your finances, stimulates healthy lifestyle choices, provides peaceful rest, fosters personal responsibility, and helps manage pain. Progress occurs when you focus on the mission. Impact agents arise, communities grow, charities collaborate, and lives prosper when a purpose transforms you. Taking off your boots doesn't eliminate your purpose—it develops it.

We are created with a premeditated plan on our lives. At inception, when the spark of life initiates a heartbeat, a moral map with a tangible destination is installed in our spirit. We're born without blinders, but they are created by culture and overcome by enlightenment. Cultural bias is embedded in every human across the globe. All are influenced by ethnicity, regardless of their own ethnicity, race, religion, gender, disability, citizenship, and disparity. However, social restrictions limit our perceived ability to navigate this map. Our destinations often reflect opportunity, but many of us don't pursue our purpose for fear of failure. Some believe that their lives are useless after reaching their goal.

There is great dissension in the United States of America regarding value of life. It often seems that only warriors understand the cost of sacrificial death. The design behind our purpose is often beyond comprehension. God may or may not allow things to happen to us. Sometimes we are victims of stupidity, carelessness, or deviance. Other times, things happen that close one door and open another. Your purpose yesterday may be different than your purpose today. Only by faith are we able to overcome that which we do not understand.

The United States is currently involved in insidious plans to legalize the murder of unborn children. Remember the sixth commandment, that murder and killing are spiritually different? Aborting an unborn child is either murder or killing, depending on the decision maker's heart. While both equal the same result for the children, the purpose of that child has already begun. Their mission starts at inception, and our decisions can determine their fate. Spiritually, taking the life of a fetus is the same as killing a child. Mothers who abort rarely forgive themselves. Like a police officer or soldier haunted for defending themselves against an armed child in battle, taking the life of another human inflicts spiritual damage. To be clear, killing unborn children for convenience is repulsive and murderous.

Does necessity negate purpose? In an ideal resolution of post-traumatic growth—being effective out of uniform—the freedom of choice personifies one's life. We often choose to remain in the moment that ended a chapter in our lives, but that's not the end. Turn the page and keep going. That tragic event will either define us or enhance our resolve. Having a purpose isn't a choice, but doing something with it is. Unfortunately, many don't know their own worth. It's often in the wilderness that we discover the truth about ourselves, and it's in nature that restoration can begin. If you do not know what your purpose in life is or you're unsure, consider doing a Survival Revival. Start peeling things away until you get to the core of your why.

Nature

Numerous studies have revealed the positive effects of nature. From healing wounds to fortifying resiliency, nature is God's medicinal creation. In 2017, Wood, Hooper, Foster, and Bull discovered that access to the great outdoors enhances mental health. With thousands of studies on green space, the evidence is overwhelming that nature is a crucial part of holistic wellness (Google Scholar). After losing his mother and wife on the same day, President Theodore Roosevelt sought refuge in the great outdoors. He believed "there is nothing man can heal that nature cannot." John the Baptist, one of the greats, lived in the wild until he was mission-ready (Mark 1:4). When Jesus took time for R&R (rest and recuperation), He found healing in the great outdoors. Nature nurtured and provided Jesus personal revivals (Luke 5:16, 6:12; Mark 1:35; Matthew 14:23). It's essential to follow this example and embark on a wilderness adventure, but remember to return to God's greatest creation—humankind.

Countless stories have been told of people becoming afflicted after spending extended periods of solitude in the wilderness. Too much of any good thing can be harmful. We're built to interact with one another, to correct one another, and to grow together. Nature forms the baseline of self-efficacy but not humanity. It is the foundation of rock on which we build our homes but not our tribe. Going outdoors is medicinal. I forged therapeutic programs in hunting, fishing, farming, survival, and adaptive adventures under the umbrella of outdoor recreational therapy. Albeit, it's important to recognize nature as only a tenth of wholeness. Although this readily available component is a platform for the other nine elements, we mustn't overdose on it.

Knowledge and culture shift with time. Humanity is ever-changing, but nature is consistent. Albert Einstein provides insight: "Look deep into nature, and you will understand everything better." Mother Teresa describes why retreating to nature is important: "God is the friend of silence.... We need to find God and He cannot be found in noise nor in restlessness. See how in nature, the trees, the flowers, the grass grow, in perfect silence—see the stars, the moon and the sun how they move in silence.... We need silence to be able to touch souls." Helen Keller helps us overcome hypervigilance: "Security is mostly a superstition. It does not exist in nature, nor do the children of men as a whole experience it. Avoiding danger is no safer in the long run than outright exposure. Life is either a daring adventure or nothing." Anne Frank touches on the healing power of nature: "The best remedy for those who are afraid, lonely or unhappy is to go outside, somewhere where they can be quiet, alone with the heavens, nature, and God. Because only then does one feel that all is as it should be." Leonardo da Vinci proclaims, "Nature is the source of all true knowledge. She has her logic, laws, and she has no effect without cause nor invention without necessity." Carlos "Chuck" Norris solidifies my point: "A walk in nature is a perfect backdrop to combine exercise, prayer, and meditation while enhancing the benefits of these activities" (Brainy Quotes, 2019). Quoting individuals from different eras and backgrounds proves the existence of a common denominator and historical consistency. We are truly equal outside because nature doesn't discriminate. She offers judgment-free services to all without the humanmade bureaucratic barriers.

Abstaining from green space is like living in a house without windows. You can live for sustainable periods, but even the most optimistic people will grow pessimistic. Fill a windowless home with family, and ruin will surely occur. Take a hike and enjoy a control-free life. Let off the accelerator and experience peaceful living.

Entertainment

Consider for a moment that you've retreated to the wilderness for a personal revival. You wander around without direction or purpose. You didn't mark your trail and left all technology at home. You have basic survival skills and focus on shelter, water, and food. Three days pass, and you begin to get antsy. Your brain shifts into overdrive, purging the chaos of life. The fourth day comes, and you're feeling philosophical. Day five approaches, and you begin to be analytical. You decide you're good to go and leave your static camp. Night approaches, and you realize that you're turned around. Establishing camp for the night is the best option to regain composure and remain safe. However, impatience sets the pace. The next morning begins with more travel, but you're heading in the wrong direction. Desperation sets in, and risk protocols get dismissed. The tall tree up ahead will provide direction. As you ascend, your body produces less energy than expected. Exhaustion and inner panic compromise your safety. *Just a little higher*, you say to yourself. A limb snaps, and you desperately grasp for another. You feel a thousand pounds heavier than before. You fall backward, quickly descending to the ground. Could this be it?

Studies cite various reasons that people who get lost perish. The top three priorities to survive are shelter, hydration, and food (with exceptions).

But one of the most important things that many forget is entertainment. Boredom, left unchecked, can lead to death. Poor decisions are as detrimental as dehydration, exposure (hypothermia, hyperthermia, etc.), and hunger. Bad choices and negative attitudes are the top reasons most search operations turn from rescue to recovery. Exercising your fortitude by embracing the situation is an effective modality of mental health training. It teaches you to remain calm in the storm (like the COVID-19 Pandemic of 2020). A volunteer with the Christian Adventure Network, Steve Claytor, is a perfect example of resilience.

A cool Saturday morning in November quickly heated up when our camp bacon caught on fire. Ten youth and their parents were attending our weekend hunting camp. My wife was cooking breakfast for everyone, Steve was preparing for the afternoon survival clinic we provide to our guests, and the rest of us were in the woods. As the bacon was sizzling on the grill, my wife was preparing other breakfast items. In a blink of an eye, the bacon became an inferno. Steve's response was epic. With a long ginger beard and ponytail to match, Steve calmly walked over to the camp kitchen, safely opens the grill, and extinguished the fire without destroying the bacon. Legend has it that his beard alone saved the bacon.

On another account, during our third annual banquet, Steve stepped up to help cater. Our caterer had backed out at the last minute, but we had a roster of volunteers and plenty of wild game in the freezer. Steve's original job was to oversee the preparation of the extreme food-eating contest, but soon transitioned to cooking everything. Steve demonstrated that he could handle himself in any given situation. He passed the test. It's important to know what people's breaking point is without breaking them. For Steve, calm demeanor and expertise allow him to lead our wounded heroes and future warriors through Survival Revivals and a Rite of Passage. Knowing when to remain static and when to mobilize is a characteristic of maturity. It's his personality and ability to procure entertainment in unlikely environments that make him so good at his job.

Wilderness survival is an extensive program for the Florida Christian Adventure Network. The impact it has on broken adults and spoiled (or identity-stricken) children circumvents long-term suffering via short-term misery. This program may sound like an oxymoron, but it is not. Each time a warrior deploys, he or she undergoes a hard reset. Without realizing it, people can become complacent in life. Many people take running water, a soft bed, personal transportation, entertainment, food made with love, their children, and even intimacy for granted. Along with these sacrifices, free will and privacy cease to exist while abroad. This time of suffering creates perspective and reveals the pettiness of first-world issues. Survival Revivals remind warriors how bad life can really be. It fosters a lifestyle of quality over quantity. Sometimes we need difficulty in our lives to remind us of how good we have it. Friedrich Nietzsche wrote, "To live is to suffer, to survive is to find some meaning in the suffering." However, the process of refocusing your spirit is achievable in a less abrasive manner (for those who are afraid of the wild).

Many therapies exist to help those suffering from hidden wounds: music, art, adaptive sports, aquatics, adventures, agritherapy, and more. Anything can be therapeutic if you enjoy it. The idea is to remove traumatic thoughts by focusing your mind on a specific task. Entertainment is instrumental in keeping the mind busy. If you can overcome anxiety by amusement, then climbing a tree will never compromise your safety.

The US Marine Corps has a saying: "Pain is weakness leaving the body" (Chesty Puller). Pain reminds us that we're alive, but it shouldn't cause suffering. It is restrictive and limits entertainment. Viewed through a lens of clarity, it can be an essential grounding point. Whether it's the pain of losing a loved one or a physical illness, it is your furnace that fortifies the walls of your spiritual compound. Physical pain often comes from being wounded or injured. Being directly involved in a situation that leads to this can result in PTSD (a form of psychological distress that is often stimulated by physical pain). As mentioned earlier, emotional pain originating from someone else's physical illness or death is secondary traumatic stress (STS). STS and PTS can produce a positive outcome if treated properly. However, allowing pain to go unchecked can imprison and cause a burden that could lead to suicide or homicide.

Many of us embellish entertainment. Instead of regarding it as a cog in the life circle, it takes the place of God. It is good to use pleasures as a coping mechanism, but they can pollute other life elements if not balanced properly. Sacrificing family to watch football, skipping work to go hunting, fishing instead of worshipping in church, and excessive gaming are examples of chronic entertainment. If God is absent in entertainment or it occupies more than a tenth of your time, then you should adjust. A review of your budget can reveal priorities.

Rest

Master the art of rest and you'll discover a door to peace. One of the most significant life elements is rest. Spec. Op. warriors are subjected to sleep deprivation in training to break them. This is also a method of torture on prisoners of war. Sleep is the one thing we do most consistently. It replenishes our spirit, heals our minds, and restores our bodies. Sleep recharges our batteries. The human body is an energy source that requires revitalization. It can make or break a person, but *rest* and *sleep* are not synonymous. Sleep deprivation is known to cause suicidal ideations, and restlessness provokes mental chaos.

Rest is part of our divine creation. There are specific life rules sanctioned by God that shouldn't be broken. The ten life elements noted in this book are those rules, but sleep is one of the most important. Sleep deprivation will drive a person mad quicker than anything else. While each of the life elements noted here can lead to self-destruction, the lack of sleep seals the deal.

Sleep can be influenced by rest-work cycles. If you have too much rest or work, your sleep will be negatively affected. It may very well be the reason that keeping the Sabbath is so important. God didn't have to rest, but He's a father who leads by example.

Everyone is a child of someone. Our parents are either present in our lives or absent from them. They can be positive or negative influencers. They have the power to shape our character. We are a result of their making, but we have the freedom to oppose. We can rebel or follow their lead, honor or disrespect them, embrace or reject them. However, just because we can doesn't mean we should. It is in your best interest to discern right from wrong, good from evil, and sin from righteousness. Often, it's in a child's nature to rebel. Only through the maturing process does one succumb to the reckoning of their ways. Many righteous parents have experienced rebellious children. Society is quick to blame parents for lousy offspring, but that's like accusing God for the suffering we bring upon ourselves. Virtuous parents are worthy of our following. They lead by example, often giving up their personal ambitions. They forgo well-deserved luxuries to aid in the development of their children's character. God, our spiritual Father, gave up His only Son for us. The least we can do is take care of ourselves by resting our mind, body, and soul to be a better child.

We go to sleep at the end of our day, but our sleep period runs into the next day. We end one day and start another while asleep. Like the seven-day week, the weekend both concludes and initiates. Theologians have argued from the dawn of our modern calendar about which day is the Sabbath. Legalistic Christians, like Seventh-Day Adventists, have it accurately pinned down to Saturday. Charismatic Christians, like those in nondenominational churches, believe any day will work because God made the Sabbath for humans, not humans for the Sabbath (Mark 2:27). Countless other religions and Christian denominations offer their insights as well. It often boils down to a convenience factor. We attend a church or follow a religion because it meets our desires. We are inhibited by our pursuit for convenience. In an effort to do more, know more, be the best, and reach goals, we have become misaligned with God's destiny on our lives. He says rest, yet we prevail in busyness. Caution should be taken not to exploit this command.

Doing too little is slothful but doing too much can be destructive. We've come to admire an overworked person and despise laziness. While corporate greed displaces many families, it is the sense of entitlement that puts us into a welfare state. Those who milk the system for "government cheese" not only devise schemes against the charitable nature of our programs but also shame their creator. We are designed for labor and benefit when we employ our skills. Sleep is good, but too much can lead to poverty. Open your eyes after resting, get back to the grind, and you'll have what you need (Proverbs 20:13). An unbalanced rest period will lead to an impoverished life because it nullifies other life elements. Without proper rest, every cog in the wheel warps.

Rest and *sleep* are not synonymous because they are uniquely invaluable. Restlessness can often stimulate incomprehensible thoughts, but an idle mind is a warrior's worst enemy. Thought training, however, can produce positive results. Although it may take several years to master, developing the ability to rest is a crucial step forward. Regenerating spiritual fortitude is key in winning this war. For many busybodies, doing nothing is often more difficult than doing something. Disappear from the outside world and reduce home operations on your Sabbath—no phone, TV, radio, news, chores, or exercising. Just you, God, and family. This break is a personal investment in your wellness. Your brain needs time to recover, so give it a break. Not only does it benefit you physically and mentally, but rest also strengthens you spiritually. Failure to "close shop" and take the Sabbath off communicates to God that you don't need Him. News flash—you do.

If you want to test this conclusion, then go camping in a bear infested forest. At some point in the night, you'll eventually give in to the suspenseful noises and pray for God's hedge of protection. Unless you give up control of self-protection, you'll not sleep. Peace at night gives way to a day's delight. Strengthening our resolve through trust in God's plan provides the essential component of healing. The scripture of 2 Corinthians 12:9 helps us understand that through our weakness arises triumph by the grace of God. In retrospect, the only way to win your war is to choose the right side. It's evident that light defeats darkness, so why hide in the corruption of this world? Let God's grace be sufficient and your weakness to shine as a testimony.

"Everything can be taken from a man but one thing: the last of the human freedoms—to choose one's attitude in any given set of circumstances, to choose one's own way" (Viktor Frankl). Rest is achievable by the surmise of Walter Anderson: "Bad things do happen; how I respond to them defines my character and the quality of my life. I can choose to sit in perpetual sadness, immobilized by the gravity of my loss, or I can choose to rise from the pain and treasure the most precious gift I have—life itself." Your cure may be a well-balanced lifestyle that's centered on God. Personal responsibility, faith, family, friends, health, finances, purpose, nature, entertainment, and rest are the ten life elements that redeem us from the spiritual virus of self-destruction.

While I'd love to beat my chest and proclaim that I'm cured, it just isn't so. The biggest flaw of humanity isn't necessarily what we can control, but that of which we cannot. Accountability and faith are the only two elements we own outright. Everything else is influenced by other people. The best we can do is choose to accept these conditions in our lives, good or bad, as a part of His plan. You see, this cure isn't a result of total rehabilitation, but the byproduct of a positive spiritual attitude.

4

SIMPLE WARRIOR

We are all created equally in spirit, but life experiences divide us. Overcoming these experiential differences challenges our familiarity. We're careful not to integrate with individuals who lack similar interests. The effort to better understand PTSD creates complex algorithms that postulate knowledge for sympathetic enthusiasts. Insight from warriors who have overcome PTS and suicide is often inconsequential. The breakthrough discovery of healing is common knowledge, but our overanalytical state of intellect seeks a more complex solution.

To those who have never served in the military, law enforcement, or fire-rescue, thank you. We would not have a job without you. This kind gesture is for the law-abiding, tax-paying, patriotic citizens who still believe in a difference between right and wrong. However, for those problematic individuals, I hope you can become better stewards of oxygen. This is me calling you out for stirring up strife. You must realize the part you play in suicides. The turmoil that self-serving citizens cause is detrimental. We can fix it, though.

Hey warrior, your life and how you live it matters. We have the responsibility of being good neighbors to one another. You produce either positive or negative energy which leads to good or bad feelings. The typical civilian spends roughly 90 percent of each day devoted to personal interest and about 10 percent of each day concerned with another person's welfare. Being discontent with ourselves is often the reason for our cruelty toward others. It becomes cyclical until we're driven mad with thoughts of rage, betrayal, and retribution. The projection of hate has nothing to do with other people but is reflective of the internal embattlement within.

Self-indulgences can cause people to project indiscretions onto others. You are inconsiderate if you fail to evaluate how your actions impact those around you. Being noisy late at night while your neighbors are sleeping, cutting someone off in traffic, not using your blinker, and stealing are examples of actions that create hostile feelings. Crowding into a hunting or fishing spot, littering, poaching, being insubordinate, ghosting someone, and other actions show disdain for humanity. Taunting and teasing are ways of releasing inferior feelings. Jealousy causes negative behavior and ruins relationships. Hate begets hate and instigating a fight with someone who can kick your butt is asinine. It's often because of rude and inconsiderate people that many suicides and homicides occur. This problem has an internal resolve. The resolution lies within each of us. Applying this formula for a balanced life prevents not only self-destruction but harm to others as well.

Most warriors need order and respect. We need you to be considerate of others in your daily walk. Don't park your vehicle in the middle of the street, be sure to say thank you when someone holds the door and admit when you're wrong. We instigate so many variables of derelict that it's impossible to count. However, we can boil each issue down and isolate the cause.

At the core of all injustices, wrongdoings, and hateful behavior is a spirit of discontent. The only way to overcome this burden is to find fulfillment in yourself. However, we must recognize that this type of satisfaction is only possible through the blood of the Lamb (John 4:14). Self-perpetuated gratification, exterior love, diplomatic peace, and materialistic joy are temporary feelings that stand on shifty sand. No religion, political banner, drug, or money—absolutely nothing provides the all-encompassing satisfaction that God provides. Without Him, you will continue to be problematic and maintain a self-destructive course that affects others.

We have popularized multifaceted algorithms to bolster our positions in global hierarchies to better situate ourselves us as nanokatal super sophisticated beings for the singular purpose of transformation. In simpler terms, we're becoming better stewards of ourselves, but we're overcomplicating it. "Keep it simple, stupid" (KISS) is an acronym I learned in the military. From A to Z, we are developing words to fit the "urbanese" language.

Communication is one of the simplest forms of resolve but has proven to be one of the toughest lessons to learn. Accountability for interaction, or lack thereof, has wrecked countless relationships. This negligence goes beyond family and friends though. Theologists, preachers, politicians, law makers and the like, seem to enjoy complicated messages. Such an example is salvation.

Aren't we tired of manipulating God's Holy Word to fit our human agendas? Exhausted from weekly messages that challenge our notion of a simplicity solution, many returns to the world for more straightforward terms. Jesus said we should come to Him like children (Mark 10:15). Being a Christian is that easy! It's not about how many souls we win, things we accomplish, or our status for public display. Rather, it's our ability to love. Love can be emulated with a smile, but even that is a struggle for some people. We are called to plow the field, plant seeds, cultivate, and harvest. Even still, most are consumers of this process. Sometimes we need to let ourselves be blessed so that others can fulfill their callings.

"Fake it until you make it" is a phrase I learned during my rehabilitation that has served me well throughout my post-traumatic growth. I cannot be sure where I learned it or if I developed it myself. It has become a common phrase in mentoring suicidal individuals and people who are struggling in life. It is a simple checkbox process to help us live life one step at a time. Life can get overwhelming. One decision can result in riches or poverty, prison or freedom, life or death. The endless temptations, expectations, and ramifications taunt us daily. It's a struggle to love hateful people. It's difficult to smile when you're hurt. However, none of these are impossible. Sometimes we must be task-oriented in our spiritual walk.

Forgive that reckless driver who just cut me off—check. Love that person who just cussed me out—check. Hug my spouse during a fight—check. Don't misinterpret the preacher's message—check. Avoid negative media that will provoke anger—check. Rebuke or remove seductive friends—check. Consider my actions' impact on those around me—check. And the list goes on. Most checkbox items are in the Bible. Please note that faking it until you make it is a temporary solution. Salvation is a formula of resolve and is the permanent solution, but it doesn't remove all our problems.

KISS has taught me how to be decisive and to make quick decisions without regret. I tend to be analytical. As a man of action, I developed a strategy to help me through tough choices. It's called the "decision coin". Sometimes I flip it more than once but doing so shows me which way I was leaning in the first place. Note that this is only for materialistic decisions. What happens in the heat of the moment when we lose self-restraint?

An undisciplined child with righteous parents will be rebuked and mentored, then relaunched for effect. It'd be nice if it were that easy for criminals. We often face years of peril, punishment, condemnation, and abandonment, which can lead to self-destructive thoughts. There's good news though - God can provide relief from this burden of human flaw. We're all broken and in need of a soul doctor. When you think of it, the world isn't that big. The problems we face are not original. Countless others have fought and won the battles we're in, but there are many who have lost. Those who won did so by being simple warriors, believing, and staying the course.

Nonprofiteering

God is, and has always been, on the move through amazing people. I can only pray, that through my present purpose, enough if accomplished to balance the scales. Church and nonprofit growth boomed in the 21st century. Charitable endeavors have become a mainstay in our society. Giving to charities makes us feel good about ourselves, grants us opportunities to be self-driven missionaries, and gives us purpose. Nearly everyone who works in or launches a nonprofit wants to make a difference. The growing number of new nonprofits is both good and bad. For established charities, redundant programs stretch local support by creating a competitive market and watering down the overall effect. Each nonprofit must complete administrative duties that are nearly a full-time job. Two different nonprofits doing the same mission require double the workforce. Warriors who develop new programs to find fulfillment can double their effectiveness if instead they join an existing team.

Nonprofiteering refers to individualistic aspirations uniting for a common cause. In effect, the competitive nature of charity combined with a hierarchy deficit requires cohesive partnerships to fulfill the global mission. Nonprofiteers are impact-driven leaders volunteering their lives to create positive social change.

Developing a program from scratch isn't easy. Surrounding yourself with innovative and selfless leaders dedicated to making our world a better place eases the burden. There is no cap on how big a team can become. If you are interested in partnering (donate, volunteer, lead, etc.), then don't hesitate to connect with a mission that complements your calling. There's a struggle to locate stakeholders who will invest in a back-to-basics program. Imagine no more suicides; no more road rage; no more anger, guilt, or hate. Envision a prescription with organic ingredients that resolves the human condition. Ten simple steps can end conflict. This solution is in your hands. What will you do with it?

Dear World

The Disney song, "It's a Small World" resonates deeply with military personnel. Deploying abroad provides an insight into the cultures on this planet, and this song captures the essence of commonality in humanity. Breaking down the walls of religious segregation, saving heroes, and building a better tomorrow unifies us with greater compassion. Giving love and understanding in a world so diverse is often our greatest challenge.

The Gospel of Jesus has spread far and wide. But even if everyone received the "good news" simultaneously, there would still be division. It is nearly impossible to be on the same page at the same time in this world because each year twice as many babies are born than people die. According to *Ecology Today* (2019), there are over 131 million births per year. Resources and personal space are dwindling. A perfect illustration is the great toilet paper shortage of 2020. During the COVID-19 pandemic that affected most of the world, civilians panicked and began stockpiling as if the end times were here. Hostilities erupted as people swarmed gas stations, grocery stores, and other first-world resources.

This chaos was an excellent opportunity to witness the transparency of self-centered motives. When a pandemic is coming, the only way to survive together is to be considerate of one another. Involving other people in your war is necessary to prevent suicide. Personal hostilities inflame our self-destructive nature, but a global pandemic is the paradox in which warriors thrive.

This antidote doesn't mean we should be blissfully ignorant to threats—quite the opposite. Shifting self-interest to interest in others is a tactical step in building your army. Being kind to others may even save you from becoming a victim. My older brother put it like this: "When you're busy looking in, you cannot see out." Self-reflecting is not the same as self-indulgence. You do not have to be a product of your environment, but it typically happens. We tend to self-reflect when we're alone, while self-indulgence increases with company. Maybe that's why I love to hunt.

Aggressive individuals need a violent release. This trait isn't a negative attribute when used for a positive outcome. Many uniformed personnel are naturally aggressive, using athletics, shooting sports, and other means to vent. Warriors can respond in defense to threats because they train to release violent feelings appropriately. However, repulsive behavior can drive a warrior to react. Beware: your nuisance behavior can appear as a hostile act. In consideration of others, and for your safety, stop the foolishness. Save a warrior—save yourself. Be kind, respectful, and considerate; that's Humanity 101. Warriors are everywhere, ready to respond at any given moment. Draw out their positive traits by being righteous.

Misunderstandings are the leading causes of hate. Hate is a thorn in your side that cripples spirituality. It is a negative feeling that breeds adversity. Don't misunderstand—warriors are not a threat unless threatened. We are a reactive force that balances your inconsideration with positive reinforcement. Your behavior reflects your true colors; words that come out of your mouth mean little in contrast. "Hating haters" is anathema to the intention of this book. We are to hate evil but love one another (Romans 12:9, Psalm 139:21–22, etc.). Cultural biases impact the way we consider one another. The path beyond human flaws is navigated by the moral compass known as the Bible. Study it, and you'll learn how to travel through anomic situations.

Cultural Constants

You can trust specific patterns of behavior when choosing your environment. In the wilderness, count on solitude. On a farm, labor is ever existent. In the suburbs of Chicago, put your money on gang activity. In the Church, you'll find charlatans and cherubs sitting on the same pew as saints. Cultural constants are evidential truths across our world. However, there are anomalies, as well—people who go against the grain, who realize that conforming to preconceived standards isn't for them. Some of these individuals break ranks as leaders. Others suffer character flaws because they're spiritually infected and have a broken compass. Skin color, origin, and gender mean little. Instead, an individual's attitude and integrity are infinitely more important. Beautiful women on television appear to be pretty. However, it isn't until you know someone's heart that you can confirm the beauty of that person.

Everyone is born with convictions, but tolerance erodes belief, and is like the Bermuda Triangle. Legend has it that countless pilots and sailors met their fate in the triangle because they lost their way. Their compasses malfunctioned. When people accept deviant behavior in their lives without consequences, they enter the triangle. Our moral compass standardizes life rules and syncs our differences. The Bible is the only book that unites humanity under the banner of love. Like the compass's 360 different directions, the Bible provides pathways for free will. Spiritual infections lead to misinterpretations, and like the triangle, they will end in death. But there's good news! A revival is coming. Not a traditional church revival, but a restoration of the Church as a whole. This is the revolutionary movement of our faith.

In the military, everyone focuses on his or her mission objective. Each person specializes in something that benefits the operation. There is no room for aberration, except when failure is at the front door. In this case, a contingency plan goes into effect. These backup plans refocus on the task at hand to fulfill the mission. Although I've witnessed methods developed by military leaders who haven't the slightest clue what they're doing, the typical reason for failure is idiosyncrasy. Individuals who don't stay within the boundaries of cultural constants for purposes of self-interest cause a ripple effect that often leads to disaster. The cultural constant within our first-responder community is courage. However, it isn't for everybody. You must find a culture that aligns with your constant. If you're afraid of dying, then you're already defeated.

Fear of Death

The fear of death is a driving factor in most of our lives. The inevitable consumes our daily thoughts. Many stop themselves short of living for fear of dying. We wait till we're near the end to begin living. Only after we lose control do we truly discover the gift of life. Tomorrow may not come, yet we take it for granted. We procrastinate a second chance with someone we love, delay completing our bucket lists, and save money for mundane things. Learn from yesterday, live today, and plan for tomorrow. Only allow death to interfere with this cycle when it is forced upon you.

The fight of your life may very well be the fight *for* your life. Everyone's external battle is different, be it cancer, victimization, an accident, or something else. Internal battles, however, are alike. Although internalized conflict is individualistically personalized based on past experiences, there is a singular aspect at play: spirituality. This baseline is what Dr. King referenced in his notion that we are all created equal. The spark of life that forces our hearts to beat, our lungs to breathe, and our brains to process isn't within our control. We cannot force a plant to grow, the sun to shine, or the world to turn. We must be good stewards of that which we're gifted.

Appreciating a gift means that you take care of it and you use it fully. You shouldn't set a gift aside but instead deploy it to serve its purpose. However, don't neglect, overuse, or abuse the gift of life. You must remember the gift-giver and recognize His intention. Death comes to us all, but life lived fully is experienced by those who are carefully fearless.

Some warriors who have near-death experiences welcome the opportunity to die for a cause. Other warriors are consciously comatose from PTS. The difference between the two is control. Fearless warriors who exercise their gift of life understand that only God is in control, whereas spiritually paralyzed warriors struggle to survive. As civilian counterparts, understanding the difference may help you become better neighbors, friends, and employers.

Recognizing the difference between external and internal battles will grant you enlightenment and empower you to be the difference in someone's life. Collaborating with your cohorts instead of competing ensures a united front against a common enemy. Nonprofiteering can be fun and daunting at the same time. Stakeholders are essential to growth and mission effectiveness. Our world is shrinking, we must navigate with the right compass. One cannot lead without proper training, love, and compassion. The cultural constants of yesterday can be different today if we elect to engage in positive social change. Being offended is counterproductive. Either you step up to influence change through love or embrace it and carry on. Spiritual warfare is frequent among many of us. Some recognize its impact, while others are blindly flailing around and being inconsiderate of others. Be strategic, be brave, and boldly live life to the fullest.

5

SPIRITUAL WARFARE

The war between good and evil rages not around us, but within. Freedom of choice often creates the internal conflict many of us experience. There are no intermediaries, mutual agreements, or unbiased ground. Either you play for the good guys, or you don't. Satan's team has an attractive recruiting campaign, but it's a trap. In a moment of weakness, when self-restraint surrenders to guilty pleasures, is when you realize how deep the rabbit hole truly goes. I hope you're geared up because we're about to launch an invasion.

Distinguishing friend from foe can be difficult. Identifying our enemy requires biblical knowledge. This book provides a battle plan. For centuries, people have attempted to discredit, manipulate, and destroy the Bible. Most have come to terms with its validity, though. "Truth sounds like hate to those who hate the truth" is a call to arms to defend our base (Proverbs 9:7-8). Behavior outside of grace, mercy, and love can be an indicator of wickedness. You must pick a side, as it is impossible to please the fleshly desires of this world and serve God simultaneously. Choose wisely; your fate and eternity depend on it.

Even the strongest succumb to temptation. Don't fret because everyone falls short. Perfection is impossible! Temporary pleasures feel good, but power, sex, adventure, popularity, and entertainment build tolerance levels that require more from you each time. Although certain desires fulfilled correctly are not sinful, they can lead to provocative thoughts. Righteousness can become sinful if it detracts from your relationship with

God. In other words, it's wrong to spend more time in the mirror than in the Bible.

Hunting, for example, is one of the purest sports around, but the desire for self-gain can create greed. Good people have become poachers because evil influencers convinced them that the laws of the land are imprudent. Hunting can be expensive, time-consuming, and habitual. It is said that your heart is where you spend your money. The same can be said about time. A wandering mind during church service reflects your heart's desire. Daydreaming about hunting, sex, work, or anything else is a pull away from God.

The difference between winning a battle and winning the war is strategy. Spiritual readiness requires intestinal fortitude, psychological conditioning (or reconditioning), and a variety of training. This chapter will help you prepare for both the battle at hand and the long-term war to come. I want to reignite and focus your warrior ethos on a combatant who's killing our heroes. This enemy will strike when you least expect it and often when you're all alone. It's hand-to-hand combat in the spiritual realm. Do you have what it takes to stand your ground?

A Lone Warrior

In a society that instills the team concept, many have lost the art of accountability. While this was spoken of earlier, the notion of personal responsibility within the confines of spiritual warfare is worth covering in more detail. At what point did we become engrossed with other people's lives when our own is in shambles? Abandoning our post to fight someone else's battle allows the enemy to infiltrate our defenses.

Maybe we search for other people's flaws as a deflection technique that dampens the blow of discontent. Uncompromised integrity can provide a stronghold of joy for lone warriors. Br righteous, even in the shadows, for in this you can rest easy.

Ownership of self is a dictator of wellness. The very thing we control is often marginalized by our refusal to recognize internal conflicts. Individualism and solidarity can harness our inner warrior to combat mental health issues. Living in harmony with one another is an external reflection of internal peace. We expect much from others, but at the end of the day, it is the self-gratifying independence that triumphs.

Do you ever wonder why Jesus spent forty days alone in the wilderness? If you read Luke 4:2, you'll note that it was to pray and fast. Fasting causes you to sacrifice desires and needs, which drives you closer to God. It provides a controlled setting to test your spiritual fortitude against the enemy. Without fasting, our abilities come between us with God. Having control is something most of us desire. If you reflect on how this impacts your relationship with others, you'll find that it can be detrimental. God wants a relationship that empowers autonomy, not one that is dictated by social supremacy.

Sacrificing desires fortifies an enduring bond. Jesus loved being around people and needed them to fulfill His mission. The text makes it appear as if He was going mad in the wilderness because of Satan's temptations. If done correctly, you too will suffer "madness" when fasting. This can be a spiritual realignment that prioritizes and rebuilds broken relationships.

We will answer for the life we choose to live. On judgment day, it'll be just you taking account for your actions. Solitude creates opportunities for us to reminisce and reflect on how it'll be on that day of reconning. Visiting past experiences can be depressing, but it can also lead to healing. Growing in relationship with the author of spirituality provides access to the commander of an undefeatable legion of warriors. You may feel all alone, but there is an army ready to do battle for you. Make the call and discover the mission of spiritual special ops.

Battle Rattle

Military personnel are issued specific personal protective equipment (PPE) before deploying. Law enforcement officers wear PPE to stop bullets, firefighters don gear to shield against flames and toxic smoke, while paramedics' PPE defends against blood-borne illnesses. PPE is designed to protect against relative hazards, so what about ministers, social workers, and mental health specialists. Spiritual illness injures and kills more people each year than any other hazard.

Warriors utilize some of the most technologically advanced equipment available. Billions of dollars are invested in battle rattle to protect us from being physically harmed. This gear proves that we are not expendable. We are valuable members of a team, our communities, and our homeland. A relentless effort goes into developing next-generation PPE to enhance our tactical capabilities, but what about our minds and souls?

The military has studied PTSD and experimented on Veterans for decades. They have refined quality care and enhanced programs to help rehabilitate warriors suffering from moral wounds. The first-responder community has recently lifted the rug to recognize and treat PTSD. Although decades behind the military, first responders now have access to best practices used for wounded warriors. Organizations like the Christian Adventure Network have stepped up to convert these services for our first responders. There are similarities between modern military combat and the situations that first responders face. While the sacrifices are different, the spiritual toll remains the same. We pay for it physically, psychologically, and spiritually.

State-of-the-art practices are now available for physical and psychological rehabilitation. The mind and body receive innovative treatment, but there is little acknowledgment of the importance for spiritual wellness. This indifference has led to a failure in protecting warriors during spiritual combat. It is indicative of our division on the matter. Battle rattle can be more than just tangible PPE; it should also protect a warrior's mind and soul. Using moral and emotional PPE requires exercise. We should spare no expense in outfitting warriors with spiritual battle rattle. However, we must first overcome the separation of church and state in this matter.

The Bible says that every knee shall bow, and every tongue confess that Jesus Christ is Lord (Philippians 2:10–11, Romans 14:11, Isaiah 45:23). Most wait for dire moments, impossibilities, or inevitable doom before seeking higher power support. Often, the most spiritual person in the group is called upon to pray. We acknowledge that person's spirituality, like the Army trusting the Air Force for air support. But independent access to God can grant you unlimited supernatural power. This connectivity doesn't happen on a whim, though. It requires an investment in relationship through training, operating, and deploying into battle.

Individual spiritual readiness can be manufactured for corporate PPE. Religion, for example, has been developed by man – for man (influenced by God). Although religion has created an abundance of good, some people use it fir personal gain. Spiritual PPE has nothing to do with religion, but everything to do with being religious (the act of repetition).

Redundancies of military and first responder training builds muscle memory and works out mistakes before deploying into the field. Spiritual battle rattled incorporates both church and state. Capitalizing on what is known in Heaven and on earth can help us create a plan of attack. Now that we know how to dress for this battle, let's discuss execution.

Tactical Maneuver

Hunting is one of my favorite activities. It is a therapeutic tool for many, a method of building bonds and tradition, a means to feed families, and a character-developing platform like none other. Learning to hunt when I was a child saved me as a man. My time in the woods enhances my relationship with God, family, and my community. It provides personal gratification and fulfills my divine responsibility to manage wildlife (Genesis 1:26–28). Hunting and gathering are natural human instincts that are not just for men (Proverbs 31:15). This is an entitlement of self-reliance, and those who cannot will depend on those who can.

The nature of hunting isn't about killing animals, it's of self-preservation. People hunt for jobs, mates, and food with similar strategies. Scouting before the hunt increases the odds of success. Locate the water hole, ready yourself, and wait for your opportunity. That which you hunt will rarely seek you out. You must know their routines, habits, and defense mechanisms to be successful.

During an archery bull elk hunt in Arizona, my guide and friend Lance Nichols revealed a fascinating strategy for harvesting one of North America's most majestic animals. Scouting, glassing, and cold calling proved to be quite useful. Locating a bull that would bugle back was rarely an issue; it was positioning ourselves to take the shot that proved most challenging. Wind, visibility, sound, and travel corridors were all considered before pursuing the bull. Both Lance and I were well trained and prepared for this moment.

We hustled to get in front of the traveling herd of nearly fifty elk as they ascended toward their bedding grounds. Within minutes of being in position, the sound of bugling bulls grew louder and louder. We sat still, had the wind in our face, and watched as the first group of elk passed just out of crossbow range. The gap between groups allowed me to maneuver into position. I snuck to within thirty yards of their trail. My crossbow was set up on a tripod, and I had a range finder in hand. The tips of my bolts were armed with razor-sharp broadheads. Everything was in place, but I watched helplessly as the next group of elk passed on a different trail eighty yards away.

No tactical maneuver could close the distance without giving up my position. I sat patiently waiting and hoping that a satellite bull would use the trail that ran in front of me. Within minutes, two vocal bulls gave up their position, and they were heading right for me. As the sound of their bugles grew louder, my adrenaline pumped harder. My teeth chattered, my hands trembled, and my heart pounded in my ears. They were so close that I could hear the saliva gurgling in their throats as they let out ear-piercing bugles. Antlers emerged from behind the juniper tree as they traversed the draw right into my kill box. The first bull was magnificent, and I knew he was a "shooter." As soon as he entered the box, I attempted to range him, but the range finder wouldn't work. He took a few steps forward, and I had lost my shot opportunity. I ranged ahead of time as the next big bull entered the box. I put the crossbow scope behind his shoulder and squeezed the trigger.

The pop of the crossbow caused the bull to leap forward and away, but the thud of the bolt didn't lie—center mass strike. But the slow speed of the crossbow delayed the bolt delivery, and it was further back than I desired. I replayed the scenario over and over in my mind. As I returned to Lance's position, his excitement diminished my doubts. After our inaudible celebration, I recapped what had taken place. His doubts that the range finder had failed proved correct, as I realized my mistake. The limbs of the crossbow had interfered with the range finder's laser. We needed to see what kind of blood was on the ground to determine how long to wait before tracking the bull, so we slipped over to the point of impact and found good blood. Within seconds, more bugling bulls were on top of us. We took cover in a nearby juniper tree, and the massive elk nearly stepped on us.

We waited an hour before setting out to track my bull. We followed his blood for a quarter mile before it ran out. I stayed on the trail as Lance began a perimeter sweep. Two hours into the track, hope emerged as Lance swiftly descended a hill, whispering for me to grab my crossbow and follow him. We stalked up on the bull that was bedded down forty yards away. Lance ranged him, and I set up for the shot. The bolt loosed from my crossbow with deadly precision.

Immediately I collapsed to the ground in tears. The overwhelming emotional roller coaster of joy, sadness, excitement, and disappointment took its toll. I was grateful to God, Lance, and my hosts and friends Sam Hiatt and Eddy Corona that my childhood dream was coming to fruition. I was sad and disappointed in myself that my first shot hadn't quickly dispatched the elk. It wasn't until a later archery hunt that I realized how much I was affected by my disability.

Military, law enforcement, and fire-rescue personnel train to provide an overwhelming offense and a strong defense. Breaching a door to fight a fire and engaging in a firefight are both highly dangerous. Years of lessons learned and tactical training reduce the risk to these warriors. Having fail-proof equipment, the ability to operate in complex situations, and knowledge of their opponents are essential elements of success. Yet we still face defeat, make mistakes, and ride the emotional roller coaster. If it were not well-balanced and in good operating order, the roller coaster could derail.

Spiritual combat training should take place before it is needed, just like any other form of preparation. Learning to hunt as a child equipped me for post-traumatic growth, but I had to translate my combat training against the Taliban to take on this new battlefield. Tactically maneuvering the physical realm can convert to help us navigate the trenches of this invisible war. It's important to note progress from lessons learned in failure. We cannot leap into spiritual combat training without first identifying how we suffer from lack thereof.

You must master tactical maneuvers before taking the fight to the enemy. The general rule of engagement is to fight one front at a time without getting outmaneuvered. Our goal is to win the war one battle at a time. This approach allows you to lose some to win it all. Spiritual warfare is no different, although many believe it is. We often feel that the big fight at that moment will determine the fate of our lives, but that is not true. Each of us is in a war for ourselves. Inside that war are daily conflicts against sexual immorality, hate, idolatry, physical dereliction, and self-destructiveness. We face many internal conflicts that can cause insolent behavior. You must fight one at a time. Otherwise, you'll become surrounded and overwhelmed - ultimately surrendering to self-destruction.

Defending your command center is the next step, but this is different than attacking. Establishing layers of defense to repel the enemy is key. Setting up defensive fighting positions allows us to fall back. This tactic provides a cushion for failure. Multiple coping strategies empowers us to stay the course throughout desperate situations. It's imperative that you developed a battle plan to defend your mind.

Basic Training

For centuries, scholars have debated the complexities of the mind and body, while theologians overcomplicate the soul and spirit. Many of us internalize these arguments to philosophize our beliefs into pliable concepts. Rationalizing our convictions against worldly tolerances can be costly, though. Friends, acquaintances, and even our communities could disavow us. But what if everyone truly lived by the motto "To each their own." Understanding your limitations can help you be influential within your realm. The greatest prayer I ever heard is the foundation of humanity. Many know the first sentence of the Serenity Prayer, but check out the full version:

> God, grant me the serenity to accept the things I cannot change, the courage to change the things I can, and the wisdom to know the difference. Living one day at a time, enjoying one moment at a time; accepting hardship as a pathway to peace; taking, as Jesus did, this sinful world as it is, not as I would have it; trusting that You will make all things right if I surrender to Your will; so that I may be reasonably happy in this life and supremely happy with You forever in the next. Amen. (Niebuhr, 1932)

Living this creed can be difficult when we're caught up in dissecting other people's lives. Returning to the basic tenants of life can realign our perspective with feasible beliefs. When an overwhelming feeling of mental chaos burdens you, when people fail you, when you're pinned down by the enemy is when your foundation proves most valuable.

Basic training for the body is simple because we easily understand that which is visible. Push-ups, sit-ups, jumping jacks, and running are time-proven exercises that can positively impact your holistic wellness. Basic exercise is a Segway to advanced training. By mastering this, you can progress to a rope course, mountain climbing, rappelling, or obstacle training. Battle carry, recovery, returning fire, and charging an enemy stronghold come naturally when you move forward accordingly. Train to perform and perform how you train if you want to succeed. Warriors know that victory begins with basic military training, so what about basic spiritual training? Is it the separation of church and state, the unwanted bias of religion, or the assumption that spirituality is an individual's responsibility which keeps us from it?

Shenanigans! It's counterproductive political correctness that hinders righteousness. As you've seen, restricting spiritual growth is disastrous. Training the mind is complicated because our inner sight is impaired. Preparing our soul for what lies ahead is challenged daily by outer-sight comprehension. Feelings are easier to understand than moral control. The mind, body, and soul are all connected through the spirit. Without this, we cease to grow. Spirituality is the lifeline for warriors. We must separate spirituality from religion, though, because religion can be oppressive whereas spirituality is liberating.

There are three phases of training: initial, advanced, and continuation. What we know now is more than what we knew before, but less than we'll know later. Even for those with commitment issues, who seek God only when in need, can benefit from spiritual combat training. Many rely on spirituality when hardships strike because it helps justify and reason the purpose behind it all.

Each military branch has a different timeline for training new recruits. Law enforcement and fire-rescue schools also have predetermined deadlines. Timelines enhance readiness through structured education. Candidates must achieve all expectations before graduation and must graduate before receiving a duty assignment. Spiritual readiness is no different. Humility, prayer, reading, meditation, love (not lust), mercy, grace, and gratefulness help balance perspective and realign morality. Becoming versed in biblical principles arms you to fight in this realm, but we must follow the rules of war.

Rules of Engagement

Spiritual conflicts reflect moral and ethical convictions. The laws of the land are designed to provide guidance and parameters like religious order. History tells of societies that refused to uphold righteous laws and then of their demise. No culture is exempt from the attack of evil influencers that shift moral tolerances. Therefore, honest men and women should take caution and be discerning to ensure that laws align with biblical standards. The Bible holds evidential truths that are paramount in spiritual warfare. This book is a database of information depicting historical trademarks, essential rules of engagement (ROEs), and a map leading to happiness and fulfillment. What other book distinguishes right from wrong so perfectly?

Our culture in America would have you believe that you can be anything or anyone you want. This has created mass confusion. Millions of people struggle with identity crises. Scientific and social truths support the notion of control, but it interrupts the divine appointment for your destiny. The saying "Just because you can doesn't mean you should" is a perfect illustration of spiritual ROEs. Attempting to trump God's design for your life always produces internal conflict. Warriors who recognize self-control as a critical process of ROEs are more likely to win their war. These rules originate from lessons learned throughout history and are bound by moral obligation. Breaking them fails to uphold superior morality. However, sometimes the enemy needs to be roughed up. ROEs that protect the wicked demoralize the righteous.

Allowing one specific moment to determine your future violates your destiny. Not everyone is cut out to be a warrior. The sacrifice and long-term commitment, the loyalty to a cause, and the undefeatable spirit fortifies your command center. It begins with standing for Bible-based ROEs. Being submissive to a higher authority is the foundation of a warrior's ethos. We must follow until given an opportunity to lead. Even then, we submit ourselves to a chain of command.

Chain of Command

Every great team has a solid chain of command (CoC). The CoC provides checks and balances to fulfill the mission. It holds team members accountable for their actions, provides ROEs, issues battle rattle, provides assignments, manages training, and harnesses capabilities for a synergistic effect. A good CoC understands that home base must be squared away before deploying abroad, while a bad CoC doesn't care about personal matters. Although this may not immediately affect the mission, it will negatively influence retention. Recruiting warriors into the Kingdom requires individual attention because each of us are invaluable in our own way.

Warriors must maintain personal accountability because the defining moment of our life originates from within. We are responsible for our actions, our attitudes, and our obligations. No matter what happens, these three things are within our control. A CoC cannot take these from you, but they can undoubtedly influence them. In my experience, leadership is often politically driven. It's rare to find someone in a position of strategic leadership who doesn't force biased agendas on subordinates. For example, the Lieutenant (LT) in Afghanistan scolding a group of soldiers who recently returned from a month outside the wire (OTW) for being out of regulation. Akin to government organizations that are strong in rules and regulations but weak in character, this first sergeant fails to recognize the futility of his ways. This LT should salute these warriors for keeping the fight OTW.

Governments do not exist to be self-serving, but they are. Like CoCs, this is the evolution of human influence. There are anomalies, though. Take Captain Benjamin Jody or Senior Master Sergeant Bill Seaman, for example. These two leaders in my CoC took fire on my behalf. They sacrificed personal and professional gain to ensure my best interest. Others reflect what a CoC should be, but they are few in contrast. Studies are beginning to reveal that PTSD can be stimulated by leadership atrocities.

Allowing others to hinder your relationship with God or your health and wellness is a conduit for self-imprisonment. If we take ownership of our lives, a CoC can be a positive attribute; but if we don't, it could foster rebellion. Leaders don't always get it right, especially when a warrior is injured or wounded in the line of duty. The military CoC appears more structured than that of the first responder community. Could this be because the military has a uniformed hierarchy at the highest levels? First-responder CoCs have more variables and influencers from different perspectives. They are led, not commanded. Imagine first-responder leadership synergistically functioning like the military.

CoCs must retain a certain level of autonomy. Each branch of the armed forces has its own CoC. Inside each department are subcommands that continue to be broken down until the lowest person on the totem pole. This system is efficient and effective. Prior military personnel are categorized as veterans. This uniformed process unites us, aids in our health and wellness, and establishes an exceptional database of reliable information. Imagine a program like that for first responders.

It is unlikely that a program of such magnitude will come into existence. The division that is tearing our country apart is also an epidemic among law enforcement and fire-rescue personnel. Jurisdiction, credit, and funding are three barriers that hinder unity. There are sensible justifications against such a notion of restructuring the first responder community. However, one may find that first responders themselves desire such a change. After all, CoCs are supposed to serve them.

Wounded

There's a significant difference between being wounded and being injured in the line of duty. Wounds occur from an enemy attack, whereas injuries happen outside of conflict. It sounds contradictory to the previous definition, but because it was not an enemy weapon that harmed me, the military classified it as an injury. They did, however, classify me as a Wounded Warrior. Two years of active rehabilitation led only to digression. I seriously considered suicide at one point, but I opted to give my life sacrificially for others. John 15:13 states that there is no greater love than for a man to give his life for a friend.

By surrendering to my purpose, I took back ownership of my life. The people who dictate my compensation no longer have control over me. I stopped blaming healthcare providers, leaders, and superficial friends for my poor health. Once I took ownership, I evolved into a mission-driven machine. My wounds no longer defined my destiny but rather fueled my purpose.

Working with countless military and first responder warriors and their spouses, family members, and friends has allowed me to gain unparalleled perspective. Studying the first responder community taught me that PTSD is a catch-all diagnosis for most mental health issues. Understanding PTSD and its impact on family members drove me to research and develop a premise on STS. Unlike vicarious trauma, which is absorbed by those who are communicatively involved, STS happens through indirect tragedy.

STS doesn't hit as hard as PTS upfront but lingers and leads to moral deterioration. A law enforcement officer who responds to a vehicle accident involving death may incur STS, whereas one who is hurt in a vehicle accident has an increased risk of PTSD. This separation is vital for each of us to understand. STS and PTS present similar signs and symptoms but treating them the same is like treating anxiety and depression the same. Both are forms of spiritual warfare, but one is treated different than the other.

Being wounded in action doesn't always result in physical impairments. Human sympathy is mostly sight driven. Physical and spiritual wounds are not comparable, for only one causes suicide. Bodily injuries are better understood because we can see them. For the warriors who suffer moral wounds, the allocation of empathy can only come from a cohort. Those who have not overcome superficial comprehension shall never realize the magnitude of such impairment. These ambiguous wounds cause suicides because they are more difficult to conquer. It's like being a prisoner of war (POW), except you're captive to yourself.

Prisoner of War

When we think of POWs, we envision horrors of torture and neglect. Being a POW may very well be one of the worst experiences a human can suffer. Part of military training is learning how to behave if taken captive by an enemy force. We learn how to survive imprisonment, evade answering questions, resist torture, and escape captivity. We also learn to create havoc for the enemy and aid in the escape of our comrades.

On a chilly March morning at Blue Springs State Park in High Springs,

Florida, I stood at attention, saluting Old Glory while Cameron Wheaton played the national anthem with his electric guitar. The sun emerged over the treetops and warmed my face. A slight breeze softly whisked the US and Christian flags hanging on stage. Midway through the anthem, another flag caught my attention. Beyond Cameron, humbly waving on a pole at the park entrance, flew the POW/MIA flag. An overwhelming sensation took hold, and I began to tear up. The epiphany that I was captive to my traumatic experience opened my eyes to the application of SERE training in spiritual combat. As I was called to the stage to speak for the fourth annual Survival Race for Heroes, I knew that my scripted message needed a serious overhaul. An opportunity to cause havoc for the enemy and help my friends escape was at hand.

PTS is imprisoning. Being wounded or injured during a traumatic situation (like war) causes internal conflict. PTSD takes prisoners, tortures, torments, and often kills our heroes. Like an enemy force that captures a soldier in battle, PTS takes spiritual POWs. This book can be an escape plan - a map to freedom. Statistics show that many who are taken prisoner by PTSD die by their own hands. In that case, should suicide be considered "killed in action"?

Killed in Action

Being killed in action (KIA) is incomparable to killing oneself. Suicide is optional, whereas being KIA during combat is on God. If you have buried a loved one who was KIA or who died by suicide, then this section may sting. Please understand that it is not my intention to cause more pain but to intercept future suicides. Suffering loss from KIA and suicide are different yet similar. There is honor and prestige with being KIA but disgrace and disappointment in dying by suicide. However, the results are the same—someone is gone. The enemy that causes a KIA is tangible, whereas the enemy that causes suicide is invisible. Both forms of death lead to spiritual wounds in those who love you. If you are thinking about suicide, remember that the suffering you're enduring is not of your own accord but an enemy force within. Self-destruction is Satan's primary goal. Don't let him win.

The enemy we face on the front line of battle is much easier to understand than the hidden enemy. Both enemies cause death and destruction, but we're only trained and outfitted to fight one. Psychological combat training can prepare us for the spiritual war to come. Instead of the current reactive initiatives designed to treat mental health issues, we should take proactive steps to outfit our warriors beforehand. The more training soldiers have, the less likely they are to be KIA or to die by suicide. Knowing the enemy's tactics is key to a successful combat op. Who in their right mind would wait to be in battle before learning how to fight?

Applying military tactics to your spiritual war can aid in victory. Learn to fight back, escape your self-destructive thoughts, and revive your warrior ethos. Don't die in vain. Stand up, brush yourself off, and join the ranks of countless warriors before you who have survived your situation. You are special, and the war you're in is unique. Nobody can truly understand because your thumbprint, your knowledge, and your life are an isolated series of experiences that only you have obtained. However, there are proven tactics to defeating the hidden enemy. Those who have learned to defend the command center repel the enemy. Note that the enemy is always ready to strike, so remaining spiritually vigilant is a must. They are waiting for you to drop your guard, looking for an opening in your perimeter, and sitting in wait to ambush you. They may give up their position to launch a mortar. Have your spiritual special forces ready to deploy. Fight on!

One of my favorite enlisted leaders, SMSgt Bill Seaman, told me when I was in a bad spot, "Get busy living or get busy dying." He knew me better than I knew myself at that moment in time when the enemy had breached the walls of my defense. He recognized the barricade I had established, like the heroic tales of Davy Crockett's last stand at the Alamo. I was under siege from a hidden enemy that infiltrated my defenses. It wasn't the constant attacks from the Taliban in Afghanistan or Al-Qaeda that had me troubled while deployed to other countries. The unseen enemy attacked me right here at home. The transgressions of hate, disrespect, injustice, greed, and hurt from people I trusted most bombarded me. I was captured and imprisoned, taken hostage for nearly five years. I was a spiritual POW, but I escaped.

Years of planning, learning the infrastructure, and waiting for the right moment allowed me to break free. The enemy forces closed in on me, like bloodhounds and marshals in hot pursuit of Harrison Ford in

The Fugitive. I was running for my life when SMSgt Seaman cornered me with a decision: stand and fight or die running. Growing up with Sylvester Stallone as my hero, this was a no-brainer. I chose to emulate Rambo and return fire. However, being pinned down in the command center required reinforcements. Waiting to recognize imminent defeat before requesting help nearly cost me my life. Delaying that long was counterproductive. The destruction caused to my moral defenses left marks that may never disappear. Like the bullet holes that remain on the walls of Ali Al Salem Air Base in Kuwait, where Iraqi forces executed military leadership in the early nineties, my hidden scars are a reminder of the battles I once faced alone. Comparable to the US cavalry rushing across the oil fields during Operation Iraqi Freedom, Jesus Christ led a legion of angels to rescue me. All I had to do was repent and believe—necessary steps in mastering psychological operations.

PSYOP

Psychological operations (PSYOPs) involve a method of redirecting or influencing individuals, groups, or governments. The big-picture name "psychological warfare" focuses on a shift in social thought. Some of you may recognize signs of PSYOPs within the United States. Anti-presidential campaigns are the perfect illustration. The media is used as a weapon in this war to tear our country apart. Frequently, those engaging in PSYOPs unwittingly circulate detrimental information. This book isn't about politics, civil matters, or international conflicts. Instead, it's about the internal war of division. It's time to shift PSYOPs from cultural manipulation to spiritual warfare. Let's take back our lives, heal our country, and unite the Church.

Everyone struggles with outside influences that steer our consciousness and convictions. Can you recall a childhood memory that changed your perspective? Parents, religion, technology, education, and friends all persuade who you become. You can attempt to do a 180, but your childhood roots will always be a part of who you are. Good parents will perform PSYOPs on their children, raising them to respect, love, and appreciate one another. Bad parents stand aside and allow others to conduct PSYOPs on their children. In either case, you have been and will continue to be on the receiving end of PSYOPs. It's your choice to repel it with intellect and maturity or to conform. Even the greatest leaders succumb to social influence. Standing your ground on biblical truths is difficult, but allowing righteousness to govern behavior aids in self-control.

The road to freedom from provocative thoughts is less traveled. Mind control, like Route 66, is well known. Few people, however, detour from their daily pursuit of success. Some have mastered self-control, whereas others need more practice. Counter-PSYOPs is a struggle. It's the art of controlling our thoughts that produces true happiness. Suicide, homicide, sex, hunting, fishing, and so forth are all culprits of distraction that keep us imprisoned. That's right—both good and bad thoughts control our present state of being. An old Native American fable puts it best.

> One evening, an elderly Cherokee brave told his grandson about a battle that goes on inside people. He said, "My son, the battle is between two wolves inside us all. One is evil. It is anger, envy, jealousy, sorrow, regret, greed, arrogance, self-pity, guilt, resentment, inferiority, lies, false pride, superiority, and ego. The other wolf is good. It is joy, peace, love, hope, serenity, humility, kindness, benevolence, empathy, generosity, truth, compassion, and faith."
>
> The grandson thought about it for a minute and then asked, "Grandpa, which wolf wins?"
>
> The old Cherokee simply replied, "The one that you feed."
> (American Indian Legends, n.d.)

Winning the war is that simple, but we continue to accept self-inflicted defeat. Feed the wolf that is just and starve the other one. We're all born into battle, but we're also born equipped with a moral conscience. Society influences righteousness through tolerance. Attractions are often a result of our environment. Typically, temptations occur from weaknesses. The enemy discovers a hole in our defensive perimeter and exploits it.

Claiming to be born a certain way is inherently right because everyone is born into sin. Most of us can choose right from wrong, but what happens when they merge? Homosexuality, for example, is a choice based on free will (1 Corinthians 6:9–10). One cannot be born with a sexual preference. We're either male or female, with reproductive organs that are inherently designed to create life. We must fight back and push the enemy out, reinforce the walls, and seek to be the people God created us to be. Those who murder have fed the bad wolf far too long. This revelation is an absolute truth that holds firm to all immoral, unethical, or otherwise sinful behavior. We must not allow society to contradict God's holy Word, and we must take caution in the distinction between right and wrong.

It is challenging to control our urges in a world full of temptation. Satan has as much power as we give him. The following section is a compilation of how some warriors personally manages temptation. In transparency, I do not always get it right. I strive for righteousness and purity, but I'm a filthy rag in comparison to Christ. I yearn for peace, but I face storms. We all fall short, but we shouldn't give up. Not even the most virtuous person can rightfully lay claim to perfection. Let's look at some everyday struggles.

Anger

Controlling anger can be difficult. Traffic used to be an unguarded trigger of mine. It seems that when people get into their vehicles, they lose all common courtesy for one another. One of my pet peeves is drivers who don't communicate, namely using blinkers. I used to be quite intolerant of rude people. Coming to terms with the fact that self-propagation creates inconsideration, is another reminder of why this book is so important. I had to isolate the root cause of my anger. Was it because of the lack of consideration for me, or was it because I had wasted my time waiting for nothing?

People who don't say thank you when I hold the door for them, litterbugs, disrespectful individuals, keyboard bullies, political assassins, greedy vultures, thieves, poachers, and two-faced hypocrites are some other examples that fire me up—or used to. I've been able to overcome anger by recognizing these things as brokenness within myself. I'm not a hypocrite - my imperfections include behavioral flaws that bother other people. Callousness to petty drama, using people's talents for the Kingdom, being conclusive, and calling out fake people has provoked people against me. I realize the plank that is in my eye and so extend grace and mercy as I hope to receive it.

Isolating the root cause of this trigger helped me overcome the anger proponent of PTS. Now, when I wait an hour past my appointment time at the doctor's office, I don't get mad. I simply let them know that it is unprofessional to schedule an appointment that they cannot keep and that I expect them to be more courteous in the future. I discovered that wasting time was my agitator. Spending three years away from my family in service to this country provoked oversensitivity to time management. Getting the most out of time is essential for me. So instead of waiting anxiously, I wait purposefully. Identifying the core reason for your anger will help you build a trigger guard.

Suicidal Ideations

Many people battle self-destructive thoughts. Some warriors are victors in this fight, many are still in the foxhole, and countless heroes will enter this war in the future. Age is a determining factor according to survey data, but it's irrelevant here. Trauma and drama are the most significant considerations for suicidal ideations. Many endure trauma, but nearly everyone faces drama. Warriors seek to identify their enemies, whereas others often fraternize with the Devil unknowingly. Suicide is a showstopper. As previously stated, it is a permanent solution to a temporary problem. Understanding your imperfections, accepting yourself for who you are, and redefining your "why" are vital in moving forward. This new norm comes at a price, though. Cutting out nouns in your life that stimulate suicidal thoughts is step one. Don't measure yourself against others; you are uniquely and wonderfully made (Psalm 139:13–16, Genesis 1:27).

Financial hardship, anomia, abandonment or rejection, instability, pain, and a silent God are excellent excuses to quit. The brain succumbs to a chemical imbalance when you're depressed or anxious. Chemical chaos can overrun your command center if you fail to return fire. You are the first and last line of defense. You must find an endless supply of spiritual ammo. When suicidal thoughts begin to seep in, fight back with an adventure. Avoid triggering thoughts by focusing on the good that is always in your midst. Grasp your why, the very reason, meaning, and purpose of your existence. Talk if you're a talker, walk if you're a walker— you know yourself best. If you're in a fog, then find someone who can remind you in difficult times. If there's nobody, then know that I am here, and I will do everything within my power to reignite your fire and get you back on the launch pad. But I cannot sustain you. That is only possible through a relationship between you and God.

Lust

Lust is an epidemic of the mind. It is predicated by the lack of self-control. One can lust for anything, but it's often in terms of sexual desire. Sex is good if done correctly. Outside influences interfere with good marital sex. Porn and dirty thoughts create an imbalance in passion for real people in your life. Lustful consideration for the opposite sex is natural, but porn makes it unrealistic. Mark Gungor (*Laugh Your Way to a Better Marriage*) does a great job of explaining this in more detail. I highly encourage everyone to glean from his wisdom.

Being alone can be detrimental if you struggle with sexual immorality, being convicted after failing to resist is a good thing. If you're not remorseful about sinning, then you're lost and bound for hell. Even religious people sin. It's the before and after that defines your relationship with God. Attempting to resist and repenting afterward are the fruits of righteousness. Our consciousness must remain in terms of black and white— this line between right and wrong, good and evil, aides in our restoration process.

The struggle is real, but God isn't to blame. He made most men sexually driven. It is natural and healthy, but we should attempt to do it right. We often fail because we allow lustful thoughts to loiter. It begins in the imagination with a kiss, an aggressive scoop, or something more explicit. Staying in your thoughts is your worst enemy. Keeping your mind busy, refraining from viewing seductive images, and knowing when you're most vulnerable will help you combat lust. When weak, don't be alone, stay off the computer, or take on a project. Even the consideration of how rampant sexually transmitted diseases are (to those who are virus-free) can be useful in turning you off.

According to the Bible, sex outside of marriage is wrong (Hebrews 13:4, 1 Corinthians 7:2–5, Matthew 5:27–30). It also states that homosexuality is an abomination (Leviticus 18:22). As a matter of fact, anything that doesn't reflect a pure heart of love, joy, mercy, and grace is wrong (2 Timothy 2:22). My point is not to burden you with righteous law but to help you identify the enemy. The spiritual enemy is desirable and causes lustfulness. Now you know what the enemy looks like, so step up and fight back.

Highs and Lows

Dealing with highs and lows can be treacherous to one's mind. It isn't easy to cope with this roller coaster, but there's a way to ease the transition from good times to bad. Acknowledging that we lack control of many variables in our life is the first step in gaining power. Determining the elements we're able to steer provides us with purpose and responsibility.

You must feed yourself before feeding others. Someone can lead you to water, but it is up to you to drink. Doing your best is controllable, whereas getting beat by someone better than you is not. Whether your destination is heaven or hell is controllable. Sinful temptations aren't controllable, but sinning can be managed by self-control. There is victory in being accountable for ourselves and trusting in God to handle the rest. Managing your business is fulfilling and surrendering to God is assuring. Cognitively understanding which battles to fight and which to give to God is key to enjoying life through both highs and lows.

For me, I dig deep and do what I can to shine my light when I'm at the top. But I know the bottom's going to fall out soon, so I remain buckled up. And when it does, I throw my hands in the air like I just don't care and embrace the ride. I often compare life to Disney's Space Mountain. Most of the time, you cannot see what's coming. The stars feel like they are within reach, but you can never quite reach them. Knowing that the roller coaster cannot last forever ensures you peace of mind that the end of your suffering is close. Spiritual endurance aids in your perseverance. Like physical endurance, spiritual, mental, and emotional stamina requires exercise. Consider the challenges that you face as opportunities to exercise. Get stronger to last longer.

Appetite

Our drive for consumption is more often psychological than physiological. Most of the time, our bodies operate on command. How we train them and how we treat them corresponds to accountable behavior. A poor diet can increase joint pain, stomach problems, depression, anxiety, and more. Eating healthy is the easiest way to reverse suicidal issues. Whole foods are vital in recovery and restoration. Dealing with appetite control is another battle.

There isn't a more practical way to exercise starving the wolf than controlling your appetite. Many have dismissed gluttony from God's law as irrelevant. A preconceived notion of gluttony is that it applies only to food. Ignoring this law allows it to overflow into other life elements, which creates an imbalance. Just as your appetite can cause you to desire more than food (sex, money, fame, etc.), gluttony and greed can drive you to suicide because you're never satisfied.

Growing up in church, I recall preachers and spiritual leaders always harping on specific commandments, laws, and biblical expectations. I'm glad they ingrained these fundamentals into my life, but I'm disappointed that they were selective. I do not remember portion control or food choice being taught to me from the pulpit. I had to learn it through institutionalized academia. We've allowed theology to manipulate us, mostly for good, but it isn't holistic. The Bible, in its entirety, voids all humanmade theology. Its instructions are precise, well-rounded, and inherently uncomfortable. We pick and choose which rules we want to follow. Convenience is our primary objective. Eating whatever we want, whenever we want, is harmful to our minds, bodies, and souls. Abstinence is commonly taught in sex ed, but we should also use it in food talk. Laziness is at the core of convenience. It takes effort to control your appetite.

The most efficient way I've discovered to control my appetite is by focusing on something else that keeps my mind and body in motion, create an eating routine, and setting goals. Boredom begets consumption, and consumption drives appetite. Desire is a product of emptiness. Emptiness is most efficiently satisfied by the "bread of life" (John 6:35).

Rebellion

Many of us are born with a rebellious spirit, though some struggle more than others. It is a natural occurrence that takes the lives of men, women, and children around the world. Death is the ultimate betrayal of effort. As a parent with two amazing daughters who are quite opposite in character, I've witnessed rebellion in both. Reap what you sow, they say (Galatians 6:7). I have struggled with rebellion all my life. That rebellious spirit is still with me today, but I've learned how to control it. I found a pivot point that helped me do an about-face, which allowed me to defeat rebellion through personal responsibility.

It wasn't when I became responsible that I began to straighten up. No, instead, it was when others began treating me responsibly. Many of us allow others to control our behavior. All I needed was for someone to trust me, to believe in me, and to give me a chance. Rebellion is often a reflection of treatment. Combating this spirit instructs us to behave like we want to be treated. Age doesn't predicate value; value is earned.

All too often, we allow other people to dictate terms on our life. The way we get treated becomes how we behave. Rejection can generate rebellion, but so can an identity crisis. When we don't realize who we are, we lean towards social iniquities. "God, I know you wonderfully and uniquely made me in your image, but this is my life, and I don't like who I am" says the untrusting soul.

Some of the best parents have rebellious children. A spiritual leader who chastises parents for their children's mistakes is blaming God for the human flaw. For us to give way to rebellion is to allow defeat in our lives. This is a battle in the war for our soul. You are responsible for doing your part in the fight, so man your post and don't worry about other people. Choose a side and commit but be wise in your choice because the Devil will lose. The wrong choice will end in your defeat.

Rudeness

Have you ever felt disrespected, walked on, or eschewed? Maybe from a stranger or someone in your group? Those who cut you off in traffic, steal your parking spot, or anger you in another way are soon forgotten. But friends or family who violate your trust often sentence you to more time in self-imprisonment.

As a Christian, I have an ethical duty to show love. I confess, though, that this love can be buoyant. Deep down inside, I am burdened with hate. This hate isn't based on race or gender, and it isn't cultural or socially formed. It's triggered by sinful behavior—I hate the enemy. I won't face this enemy on a traditional battlefield, though. As a matter of fact, I don't hate the Taliban or Islamic radicals who fight for what they believe. I don't hate illegal immigrants who sneak into our country. I hate the demonic forces that take inherently good people and twist their minds into provocative beings, into people who have little regard for fellow humans.

Self-indulgences serve a temporary purpose. Greed, mendacities, impertinence, abhorrence, haughtiness, and self-destruction describe a few wicked spirits, but the list goes on. These are spiritual infections that create conflict between us. Those who recognize these fallacies and take corrective action are on the road to heaven. Those who realize the errors of their ways and embellish them are risking hell. I don't need to reference a specific verse in the Bible because it's full of scripture that confirms this bold statement. It's the truth that is buried in the name of tolerance and acceptance. It is cowardice to fear sinners, and Christians who conform deny Christ. Your stance doesn't have to be as bold as mine, but you should hold the line. The enemy slips past your position as you slumber in your foxhole. They have infiltrated and are sabotaging our belief in God. Hate is an infection that rots the soul, and rudeness is the stimulant.

There is a lot of traveling, cultural immersion, and human interaction in my line of work. As a social scientist, I witness a variety of behaviors. I once thought that situations reveal people's true colors but have come to realize that behavior predominantly reflects people's spiritual wellness. We tend to project our states of mind onto other people. That is why written communication is more challenging to emotionally decipher than verbal communication. People make assumptions based on their internal feelings at the time. Nonverbal interactions during road travel often lead to misinterpretation. Those who give the benefit of the doubt are typically more at peace with themselves than those who assume hostile intentions. However, this isn't always the case, especially for warriors who are trained to read posture.

While traveling over 250,000 miles and interacting with over a million people, countless situations have occurred that enlightened my view on the human condition. One incident remains fresh in my mind. As I was leaving a business meeting at Blue Spring Park in High Springs, Florida, I was traveling down a dirt road. I slowly approached a white car creeping down the exit lane. I kept a two-second gap, close enough to let them know I would like to pass if they would be so kind, but not so tight that they felt threatened. The car reduced its speed and straddled the road. I gave it a minute and then backed off to a five-second gap. It took forever to get to the pavement, but once we did, I quickly took advantage of an opportunity to pass.

As I attempted to pass, the driver also accelerated. We went from thirty to seventy miles per hour within a matter of seconds, and oncoming traffic was approaching. I felt threatened and a strong urge to run the guy off the road. But I noticed a child in a car seat and quickly submitted. As we approached a stop sign, I pulled up beside him and rolled down my window in hopes he would be brave enough to converse with me. He wasn't, so we went our different ways.

In a post situation evaluation, I tried to uncover instigating factors. The man was probably having a rough day and looking to be spiteful. However, his perception of the situation may constitute another angle. His failure to yield jeopardized not only my safety but the life of his child as well. Engaging in combative tactics with me triggered a defensive response. We're both fortunate that I found the "off switch." The interpretation of such a situation is always in the eye of the beholder. Everything in our lives came to a head at that precise moment. My love for children will always triumph over hate for the enemy.

Experiences and current drama can manifest themselves in a moment of haste. Some warriors have experience in these situations, while others are rookies. In both cases, it's best to remove yourself from the situation. It may take minutes, hours, or days, but you'll soon get over it. If you take unnecessary action in the moment, you'll live with the consequences for the rest of your life. Be sure that you don't unknowingly approach someone who is armed or well trained in hand-to-hand combat. They may punch your ticket. You may be the triumphant one at that moment, but you'll be the ultimate loser as you consider your actions behind bars. The first person to initiate aggressive behavior typically loses.

My friend Tony Dilello and I were discussing the horrors of Gainesville (Florida) traffic. He revealed that he too used to struggle with combative driving. But when he became a Christian, he found peace and understanding. Tony described how he used to live in the fast lane and was always pressed for time, but with his salvation came calm. His anxiety was removed, the burden lifted, and what he once considered a threat he now viewed as moronic behavior. He cruises in the slow lane and watches as people jockey for position. He listens to a local Christian radio station (Joy FM) and shows up to work happy. This peace, in turn, exemplifies his testimony with the employees at the car wash. One man's salvation can impact thousands of lives.

Tony has a divine purpose to influence people's lives. His value to the Kingdom and our community is incomparable. James Coates is another impactful convert. He invented lightweight and inflatable armor for military and first-responder personnel. When he spiritually transfigured from self-serving to purpose-driven, he became an icon of hope. Known as the Tony Stark of Gainesville, James launched a charity called Superheroes for Hope. Positively impacting the lives of his employees wasn't enough. His salvation drove him to do more. Although he has come under countless attacks, as every Christian does, he has maintained a balance between fleshly temptations and spiritual victories.

It is tough for a combat vet to accept the terms of turning the other cheek. We're used to returning fire, standing our ground, and taking it to the enemy. Rude people violate us physically, emotionally, and spiritually. Their verbal and nonverbal interactions, moral atrocities, ethical violations, sexual exploitations, jealousy, and hatefulness are a slap in the face. Our initial reaction is self-defense; our response is retaliation; and our motive is to eliminate the enemy. But are rude people your enemy, or are they conveniently flawed for your spiritual training?

Loss

Loss happens! We gain, we lose, we gain again, and we lose again. So goes the cycle of life. One of the greatest calamities ever recorded is the story of Job. It is the tale of a perfect man. Job was righteous in the sight of God, honored among men, and feared by Satan. Job had the "American dream." He wanted for nothing, but in the blink of an eye, all that he had was lost. His entire family was murdered. His homes were destroyed by natural disasters. His business assets were seized, and employees executed. The only thing Job had left was the clothes on his back, his life, and a few judgmental friends. Even though he also endured poor health, he remained spiritually intact (Job 1:20–22).

To date, I have not even come close to suffering like Job. I cannot express empathy in such a way to connect. However, I do not withhold my compassion for those who have. My shoulders are saturated with tears. I carry the burden for many, as most ministers do. To push forward in loss, I have learned that one must move beyond their understanding (Proverbs 3:5). Know that He will wipe away every tear from your eyes. In death there is life. All pain and suffering will cease and desist (Revelation 21:4). While many evangelists have popularized John 3:16, Romans 6:23 should be our inspiration for hope. The good news is that Jesus conquered death. It is okay to mourn for your lost loved ones (Matthew 5:4). Do not abstain because it will catch up with you. There is no immediate cure for loss, but time can heal.

In the moment of such suffering, that raw piercing pain which riddles your torso and cripples your legs, debilitates joy. Nobody expects happiness, but your sorrow must not linger. Get back up and push forward. You still have purpose, and your team needs you. Knowing your value should be an antidepressant. Don't abuse drugs, abstain from excessive alcohol use, avoid sexual immorality, and accept the gift of life.

Dealing with relational breakups, divorce, friend-snipping, and abandonment can be extremely difficult. Often, these are psychologically catastrophic because we internalize blame. The situation is both controllable and controllable. You can only control your actions. Nothing is irreversible but death (speaking in the flesh). Most of the time we suffer broken relationships because of pride and arrogance, ours or theirs.

Self-indulgences can also cause this loss. So can disobedience, lack of loyalty and commitment, and so on.

Many people commit suicide because of relational dissention. The feeling of controllable helplessness creates a swift moral decline. Time heals those mourning the loss of loved ones, and so shall time remedy rejection. I'm all too familiar with this pain because I have suffered in this area considerably. Focusing on tomorrow's triumphs gets me through today's tribulations. Depression happens when you can't escape yesterday, and anxiety occurs when you're too far into tomorrow. Now, here, at this moment, is your life. Enjoy those in your presence and live in the now.

Inadequacies

Have you ever heard the phrase "We're our own worst critic"? Overcompensating for a handicap can throw you off balance. Using a disability as a crutch is welcome among sympathizers but repulsive to empathizers. Most charitable endeavors are public relations driven. Many who are "helping" wounded warriors, homeless individuals, and underprivileged families have something in common: they enable the circumstance. Pacifying the situation with handouts, freebies, and coddling may give the provider satisfaction, but it is detrimental to the main objective. To truly help is to provide opportunity, empowerment, and hope.

My mother taught me that if I worked for something, I would appreciate it more. Life requires a daily effort. We cannot stand on the mountain top without fighting off the opposition. When I was a child, my older cousin, big brother, and I would play king of the mountain. I rarely won. But I learned an essential life lesson: work harder to get better by competing against people who are smarter, tougher, and more popular. Winning against someone who is lesser does not advance your ability.

Chronic pain from invisible injuries is difficult to understand. It is a worthy adversary. A physical disability requires lifestyle adjustments, but an emotional disability can impeach your soul. You must accept the terms of your limitations to remain adequate. Inadequacy occurs in defeat. Take steps to own your new normal; don't let it define who you are. Discover what you can do by disavowing what you cannot do. Adapt, overcome, and carry on. Focus on your abilities, not your disabilities. Learn adaptive strategies to continue forward. Nothing is impossible unless you accept the terms of defeat.

> Let me tell you something you already know. The world isn't all sunshine and rainbows. It is a very mean and nasty place, and it will beat you to your knees and keep you there permanently if you let it. Nobody will hit as hard as life. But it's not how hard you hit; it's about how hard you can get hit and stay standing. How much you can take and keep moving forward. That's the champion spirit. Now, if you know what you're worth, then act like it. You must be willing to take the hit, and not point fingers. Cowards do that and that ain't you. You're better than that. (*Rocky Balboa*)

One of the most challenging things about hidden wounds is the requirement to prove their existence. This repetitious requirement is counterproductive. Being a slave to the compensation-and-pension program hinders the healing process. You must make an impossible decision: either work to get better or work to get benefits.

Compensation and pension is a debilitating process that will monetarily punish you if you get better. You must be willing to accept the terms of this game to win. Ultimately, your goal is to exterminate the spiritual infection that causes poor mental and physical health, to have quality of life, and to serve a purpose higher than your own. To get beyond your disability, you must be rebellious to the process. Your experiences are invaluable. Everyone has something to offer, but are you willing to endure the repercussions of escaping enslavement? Stephen Hawking is the most famous example of my point. Your disability doesn't make you inadequate; your attitude does.

Lying, Cheating, and Stealing

Lying, cheating, and stealing are signs of a deeper moral conflict. Damnation starts as a microscopic virus that allows spiritual infections to take hold. Telling a noble lie, cheating to help someone, and stealing from the rich to give to the poor are oxymorons that void the good of your intention. These are deviant characteristics that flaw the baseline for moral character. Righteousness cannot stand on a cracked foundation. It is a sign of cowardice and portrays a lack of respect for those around you (situationally debatable). The first time is a prelude for many more unless you allow conviction to alter future decisions.

Social tolerances inhibit moral value. Accepting them enables spiritual infections that become habitual. We begin lying to ourselves to justify constant manipulation. Some say that a little white lie never hurt anyone, but it is a bullet hole in your soul.

As a kid, I would repurpose empty milk jugs, fill them with water, and use them for target practice with my BB gun. As I shot tiny holes into the jugs, water would begin to leak out. The more holes I placed in the jug, the quicker the water drained. Eventually, the container was empty, and I couldn't refill it without first sealing the holes. As I pondered on ways to patch them, several quick-fix attempts failed. I realized that the only way to repair the damage was to purge, purify, and cement a substantial element that would hold under pressure. It took time to do this, though, and as a child, I lacked patience. I wanted it done right then and there.

Repairing the jug is like mending our lives after suffering years of lies and deceit. It takes time to get our command center in shape. Being forgiven and receiving salvation are instant, but that doesn't fix the damage we caused. That's on us! We must actively engage in the pursuit of righteousness. The temptation to lie, cheat, and steal may linger and tease you from time to time. Combat it with satisfaction in your salvation. Every time you speak a lie, imagine that you gave permission to a Roman solider to lash Jesus.

Lying, cheating, and stealing are synonymous sins. Each robs you from growth, prosperity, and relationships. People, like me, view these behaviors as enemy aggression. We build a wall for protection to keep these shenanigans outside. This defensive measure reflects God's perspective on moral violations. I once struggled with these spiritual infections, as many people do. But in 1999, something significant happened – I met my wife. I have not intentionally lied, cheated, or stolen since then. I no longer struggle with this desire because I hunted down and slayed this rabid wolf.

My redemption comes from a single source: the blood of the cross. Instead of desiring to take, I yearn to give. Faith, family, community, and country are in harmony when we rid ourselves of this wolf. Being a liability is a choice, but so is being an asset. Do you have the guts to be trustworthy?

Violence

Savagery has been around since the dawn of time. Humans are the only creatures that can control violence through morality. It would appear, however, that certain cultures are less vehement than others. We always have a reason to fight because we're naturally ferocious. Violence is often a necessary evil to combat wickedness. Some may consider unification as the final solution for peace, but they would be wrong (in the worldly form). Muslims unite under the Koran, yet violent attacks occur among different sects of Islam. Black-on-black crime is rampant because, in my opinion, the common enemies of enslavement and segregation no longer exist. Tribes battle for land and resources, and political assassinations transpire within the same parties. There are zero worldly exemptions from violence.

The goal to unite the world under the banner of Christ will continue to fail because of sin. First-world governments refute this supernatural power that overcomes deviance and violence. From the superpowers of globalism to our very own homes, sin has become whitewashed for acceptance. This tolerance in turn creates division. The most substantial and evidential reason to unite still begets segregation. Christianity is black and white, yet we have devised reasons to disagree. This split is cause for concern. We, as the body of Christ, must overcome dissension among religious ranks to bridge the great denominational divide.

It is impossible to unite in the flesh because we are inherently violent. Be it in the physical or spiritual form, many people struggle with violent thoughts. However, there is a solution. Unconditional love, something that we struggle to comprehend, can conquer violence. This type of love has no expectations, no limits, and no comparable force. But I must warn you—it is both obedient and sacrificial. It demands humility, surrender, and all worldly possessions. We have demonized this concept out of fear of being at a disadvantage, but what if loving unconditionally created an advantage for peace and happiness? We are only as valuable as the merits of our actions.

Those with divisive spirits will seek to discredit the effectiveness of unconditional love. The human condition of violence is both despised and sought after. It is addicting, and we're hooked. Furlough those thoughts for now and stretch your perspective to consider the possibility that cultural normalcies contain sinful manipulation. We are, after all, products of our environment.

Transforming your process of thought is vital in spiritual warfare. We are in a crisis of mega proportions, a disaster area where relief workers are treated with contempt and considered irrelevant. We must identify the culprit, the perpetrator who comes to confuse and destroy. You may find yourself cursed, hated, and spit on if you choose to unite with Christ. It will require a rebellion to self-efficacy, an unhindered perspective, and a relentless desire to awake Jesus. Until we've conquered hate through love, there will always be violence and division. If you are experiencing these things because of who you represent, then you're getting life right. Emotional and physical pain hurts worse in the beginning, but as time goes on, it tends to lighten up. Yet the question remains: how can I combat violence without being violent?

First, remove yourself from the environment that breeds hateful thoughts. Stop viewing movies and media that romanticize violence, cease listening to music that provokes it, avoid virtual combat (online arguments), and saturate yourself with negative ions. Second, figure out a safe way to vent. For me, this is hunting, fishing, chopping wood, shooting, martial arts, wilderness survival adventures, farming, and adaptive sports. Working out, extreme adventures, and sex helps too. So does a glass of wine at dinner.

Each of our roots are different, but violence affects us equally. It is a disease that attacks our spirit. Third, practice unconditional love. Loving to this extent doesn't come easily. Naturally, we want to hold onto things; remembering the hurt helps avoid future wounds. Stopping violent thoughts requires supernatural intervention. That cannot happen without your permission. God gave you free will to choose Him or Satan. There is nothing in between, no mutual ground, no unbiased sides—only a thin line on which you cannot balance.

Humility

As we condense the human condition to resolve the internal turmoil that embattles each of us, we come to the actionable character trait—humility. For some, meekness comes naturally. For others, it develops over time. The number-one teacher of this life lesson is failure. Death, disability, and defeat are the three D's that mold self-effacement. Arrogance is a disgusting trait that fosters dissension, division, and insubordination. Those who struggle with it either don't realize their behavior or merely don't care. Arrogance is the belief that you're better than everyone else, that you can do anything without assistance. Life is impossible without outside help. Haughtiness can lead to suicide. Committing oneself to humility means accepting the hand you're dealt. The fuse of self-destruction is lit by the notion of impossibility and executed by the proponent of control.

Humility is a cost worth paying for ones' sanity. Imbalance creates confusion about who's really in control. God has the reins of my ten life elements, though I'm the steward of my fate. I'm a newbie at life, a rookie destined for mistakes. Humility is a characteristic worthy of God's attention. Children who think they know everything are often given enough leeway to make mistakes. A good parent will be there to catch them, though.

Deflection is an excellent technique for exercising humility. Most of us want credit for the things we do. Great leaders give the credit for their success to those around them, whereas weak leaders blame their failures on everyone else. It is tough when your effort is in vain, discounted, or credited to someone who is undeserving. This violation creates a feeling of worthlessness, helplessness, and otiosity. The issue here isn't principle but spiritual. God is omniscient, and He knows your every move. If you want to win the spiritual war, then you must come to terms with the fact that earthly credit is irrelevant. Power, position, and fame do not stop suicidal ideations; humility does. Caring about what other people think has led to countless suicides. Jesus didn't try to win religious approval. He spoke the truth, walked righteously, and maintained a steady course to His destiny. Submitting to Him was my first step in humility.

Christianity 101

Christianity is love, grace, and mercy. Anything that does not reflect a Christ-like image cannot qualify. This devotion is not religious; it's relational. Religion is the theological breakdown and interpretation of historical values, whereas relationship is obedience and faith in a mutually beneficial friendship. There is nothing wrong with being religiously devoted to a relationship. There are, however, rules and restrictions to Christianity that one must follow to ensure sanctification. Many confuse these guidelines as religion, but these are relationship protocols for every friendship. Relationships are gifts that require effort, and so goes salvation. There is law in all goodness and lawlessness in all wickedness. Let's cover ten basic principles:

- Christians are humans too, we make mistakes. Confess, own it, and try not to do it again.
- Forgiveness is freedom. Relinquish your jury seat and enjoy life.
- Theology can create segregation. Don't allow your education to foster division.
- Only love can defeat hate. Anything else is akin to shooting blanks.
- Remodel your communication - speak life.
- Identify sin and resist it. Master your five senses.
- Be a caregiver for the temple of God. Nurture and tend to your body as a holy vessel. Give it proper fuel for optimal performance.
- Accept the gift of salvation. God forgives you; now forgive yourself.
- Don't be fake. Shallow Christians do more harm than good. Follow through!
- Be considerate of others in all your ways. Don't be a stumbling block by the way you dress, drive, occupy space, consume matter, and so on.

This list is not all-inclusive but is an example of unacceptable human behavior that is rampant in society. I'm asking you to be super-human because it's possible. Self-indulgences degrade your relationship with God. Every one of us is made in His image. We're His greatest creation. To treat others unkindly is to insult Him. Be like Christ—a friend to sinners. However, be careful not to get drawn in. Maintain a life in the light, crossing the gray only to rescue people from the dark. The gray is the enemy line. If you get captured behind enemy lines, remember what you learned in this book. Lean on memorized scripture. Survive and escape, or signal for rescue.

Oswald J. Smith wrote, "Oh my friends, we are loaded down with countless church activities while the real work of the church, that of evangelizing to the world and winning the lost, is almost entirely neglected." You don't have to attend church to have salvation; instead, you become the Church. The Church assembles to fulfill our duty in praising and worshipping God, to recharge and fuel our spirits, and to fellowship with other believers. There is no such thing as permanent Christian solitude. When truly saved by conviction and understanding, our hearts and minds transfigure. We desire community with other believers. If you struggle with this, then go back to the drawing board and reflect. You'll discover that there's a seed of discord choking out your mustard plant, soil depletion in your garden, a pine beetle in your lumber forest, or hidden cancer slowly eating you away. If you hold dissension against other believers for one reason or another, you may have the spiritual virus. It's time you make an appointment with Dr. J. Christ, the Son of the Alpha and Omega, Mr. Perfect Himself. It's time to be a real Christian. Leave your agenda at the door. Show up early because He's not like our medical community, which overbooks for profit; He'll see you on time.

We are to be beacons of hope, like a lighthouse which is a permanent structure that withstands the most horrendous storms. Placed in areas that are known to be catastrophic to vessels, shining brightly through the darkest hours and piercing the fog with a mighty sound. We become lighthouses when we receive Christ, but many believers only shine their light inside a well-lit building—the church. This behavior is anathema to the Great Commission (Matthew 28:16–20). If you always show up to eat but never work it off, you'll grow fat and lazy. If you never show up to eat, you'll starve. Figure out your balance, give and receive, and unify the body of Christ in harmony, humility, and love.

Broken Relationships

Caring about people comes at a cost. If you trust, you'll eventually get burned. Loving will inevitably beget hurt. Loyalty leads to abandonment.

As the saying goes, "All good things must come to an end." I would give a thousand hurts to experience love once. It is, after all, the most powerful force in the world. But why do relationships fail? In my experience, there are five sure reasons why people don't get along:

- indifference
- misunderstanding
- skepticism
- drawback
- divinity

God created each of us for a purpose. Not one single person was conceived without reason: God doesn't make mistakes. Sometimes, though, our goals are irrelevant to others because they don't line up with their own life mission, and that's okay. It is merely an indifference that we can choose to overcome or ignore. For military members, we struggle to adjust to civilian life because we're not used to trivial matters. I don't mean this as an insult to civilians but as a compliment to veterans. Indifference will cause dissension if we fail to overcome the misunderstanding of differences.

More times than not, relationships fail because we're not willing to grind through misinterpretations. False perceptions are often deal busters. To work through our differences in pursuit of common ground is humane. The sun is up in America, but it's nighttime in Asia. Both are matters of fact, but if one person doesn't communicate his or her position, then it all falls apart. Law enforcement officers want compliance and obedience. Although there are irregularities to this (officers abusing their power), the typical escalation occurs because of skeptical pedestrians. Take a minute to put yourself in their shoes, then you'll understand.

Skepticism occurs because we restrict the boundaries of our minds. We don't believe because of our experiences, our education, or our guilty conscience. Suspicion arises when someone misunderstands and doesn't provide an opportunity for the other party to overcome. Most law enforcement officers serve to protect their communities. They want to establish a safe and peaceful world. Unfortunately, they are bound by oath to enforce laws that are often enacted by greedy politicians—or so goes our theory that feeds skepticism toward law enforcement. Rules are a drawback to living in a free world restricted by order.

Relational drawbacks occur when one party is more consuming than the other. The more I call on someone, the more valuable they are to me. This factor is often misconstrued as neediness, and people can get tired of helping. But I am spiritually needy. In a sense, I cannot change the world without the world's cooperation. A movement requires people to buy in, to act for that cause. The most significant drawback that I deal with is individualistic aspirations. There is nothing wrong with individualizing your life, but we all must join a tribe. The lone wolf stands a better chance of surviving in a pack. But to join the pack, they must be willing to set aside their self-proclaimed leadership positions until the time is right for them to move up. They must accept differences, humble themselves during misunderstandings, and put in the effort to overcome skepticism. However, a humble lone wolf may remain in solitude for a season of life by divine intention.

In my opinion, God, through the Holy Spirit, influences people to come into and go out of our lives. This wisdom is where "reason, season, or lifetime" comes into play. As previously mentioned, friends come and go throughout your life. Some are there for a reason, some stay for a season, and some remain for a lifetime. Trying to understand and predict which friends will do what will drive you insane. Just go with it, do your part, show yourself friendly, and recognize the five most common friendship busters.

Remember, you can only control what you do. It takes two to tango, and friendship requires maturity and acceptance of each other's differences. Forgiveness is vital, but so is understanding. Broken relationships happen because one party refuses to work through issues. They would rather walk away than confront the situation. This is gutless behavior and reflects relational irresponsibility. Ignoring someone is for the weak and cowardly. Friendship requires work, and those who are willing to embrace the struggle are the courageous ones who will remain by your side through tough times.

6

BATTLE BORN

B eing born again is often defined by a momentous occasion that resurrects spirituality and purpose. A new lifestyle emerges with a premise on priorities. For the Christian convert, it typically means surrendering control, fleshly desires, and worldly possessions. Those who genuinely devote themselves to God find sanctuary in spiritual autonomy. They join the ranks of an undefeatable army through a recognizable change that manifests joy, peace, and freedom. Many accept trauma as a pivot point in their life. Find comfort by surrendering the outcome of your life to God by accepting Jesus Christ as your Lord and Savior. The impunity of our efforts can now have eternal results. Anything outside of kingdom work is done in vain. But what about those few who are reborn through battle?

Nearly every believer can recall the day they were born again. That moment when conviction overtook them, probably at their lowest point, when they yearned to live free from the hefty burden of life. That moment in time is your pivot point that initiates a new sense of direction. The same is true for our warriors who are "battle born"—purged through combat and fortified in fearlessness.

During the initial stages of rebirth, Christians and warriors must relearn to walk. New Christians often battle habitual tendencies, while warriors battle PTS or other impediments. Both are demons of our own design. Warriors who are battle born suffer through an intense healing process. They labor with organizations and people fighting for and against them. The worldly struggle for exceptionalism is overwhelming. Everyone wants to save warriors from themselves, but all who strive outside of spiritual restoration do so with shallow effect. Bandages are useless without antiseptic.

Our country toils day and night for the solution. Researchers spend billions of dollars and countless hours trying to discover what is already known. Some may discard your cure as irrelevant because it's not tangible or measurable. These same skeptics would've doubted the Wright Brothers' claim to defy gravity. The remedy is already inside each of us. It is a deep well that is ready to be tapped. Being battle born means nothing if you're not born again. Tap that well and mark this day as the renewal of your mind, body, and spirit. Now's the time to move forward. Let's take the fight to the enemy.

Moving Forward

Warriors on the front line of battle understand the necessity of taking ground. It is the paradigm of triumph. Legends depict courageous leaders standing up amid overwhelming enemy forces, rallying their troops, and charging head-on toward likely death. This heroic behavior has a small window, though. Timing is everything! If you move forward prematurely, you'll get cut down. If you freeze up, the enemy will flank you. The opportunity to press forward is the difference between chance and inevitable failure.

Fear is the result of uncertainty. The warrior who overcomes fear finds promise through courage. This promise is of everlasting life, of value in death, and of legacy. It is unknown how many souls have given their lives in the name of freedom. Countless undocumented martyrs have gone before us whose names are lost in time. But historical records don't capture everything; heaven does.

In an era when documentation seems omnipresent, we spin in the whirlwind of desire to capture our best moments on video. We seek recognition, yearn for popularity, and strive to become leaders who stand out. We want our names to mean something, our lives to matter, and our deaths to count. We measure our success against those mighty men and women who have gone before us. We attempt to emulate their courage, but records show that their courageous acts arose in unique situations. They dared to stand up and unleash a battle cry in the face of the unknown, but their legacy isn't solemn. Their acts of valor would be in vain if they hadn't rallied troops from their foxholes to follow them into the fight.

Moving forward requires timing, trust, and faith. Patiently awaiting the right moment to rise up is difficult in a world of instant gratification. Trusting your support team to follow you into battle is difficult. We wish it upon nobody but ourselves—a form of punishment for getting it wrong.

We don't want company because it's tough to communicate while under duress. Talk is cheap, and our moment of chaos is indescribable. There's nothing you can say to make it better, and nothing will flow from our lips that will not count against us. The right moment to move forward often occurs when we're all alone. There's nobody to rally, no troops in the foxhole, just you taking fire all alone. We're in a moment of abandonment, or so we think.

Faith is a proponent of personal integrity. It defines our ability to move forward under fire when we're by ourselves. It is the comprehension that our moment means something. It encourages us when there's little hope. It is always available but sometimes hidden far behind a tragedy. Void of the five senses, faith requires us to ponder the sixth sense—a feeling, an emotion, a vibrant appeal of motivation. Hope is an element of the Holy Spirit. With faith, hope thrives. But what happens at that moment when you move forward and strike an improvised explosive device (IED)?

The New Norm

A burning sensation runs down the back of your head, accompanied with a sharp pain in your neck. Your ears are ringing, and your head is heavy. You're face down in the sand. You can hear echoes of gunfire, explosions, and people shouting. You struggle to bring your arms into position to push yourself up, but you find that they won't cooperate. Your heart is racing, and your pulse pounds in your eardrums. Suddenly you feel yourself floating. You slip in and out of consciousness, envisioning your loved ones back home. You awake, now facing the sky with your battle buddy coming in and out of focus. Your team surrounds you, but words are difficult to speak. You drift off and awake under a bright light with white coats all around. People are scurrying, and you can hear loud, sharp clinks from medical equipment. Oblivion takes hold, and you return to a deep slumber. Only to be awaken by the sound of roaring aircraft engines. An airman in a flight suit walks by. You doze off again, this time waking to the continuous sound of beeping. Your room is bright, and you're all alone. You fight to move but your heavy eyelids and lethargic muscles won't give way. You surrender to the inevitable.

The sound of your heart monitor beeps in the distance. A sweet, recognizable voice caresses your ears. As you open your eyes, you see the one who kept you going during the deployment. You feel her soft touch on your hand and greet her gently. She's all teared up and emotional. You check your extremities and see that all four remain. The doctor enters the room and reveals the damage: traumatic brain injury, a fractured C-spine, and some remaining shrapnel. "You're one lucky guy," the doctor exclaims. A military representative soon follows. You inquire about the incident, seeking a SitRep (situation report) on your team. The representative withholds details about your unit but enlightens you on the event that caused your injuries. Details are scarce, and his nonchalant attitude frustrates you. Weeks go by, your loved one remains at your side, but the military refuses to debrief you. Frustration leads to anger, and you begin to lash out at your wife. A military chaplain visits and sits down beside you. His news isn't good. Your team took a heavy loss. Three were KIA, including your battle buddy who rescued you.

Guilt floods in and depression fills your gut. Anger turns to wrath, and you lash out at everyone who enters the room. Your spouse is unable to withstand your brutality, and she leaves. You want to return to the fight as soon as possible, but the military refuses your request. You spend months in rehabilitation, eager to return to duty, but discover medical retirement orders awaiting you. You go through the motions of leaving the military, but you're not paying much attention. All you can think of is vengeance and redemption, but that's stolen from you. You're angry because you slept through the funerals of your battle buddies. If you wouldn't have tripped the IED, if you were just strong enough to stay in the fight—"*if*" lingers and eats away at your soul. *Was I the reason? Have I become a liability? What do I do now?*

Transitioning from military into civilian life can cause catatonia. Very few people have similar life experiences. You listen in disbelief as grown men complain about petty dilemmas. Self-ordained leaders and counselors attempt to mentor you, but they haven't walked your mile. People want to help, but they don't know how.

Your need is too significant, your ask too great. You refuse to request help in fear of denial or owing someone something. The organization that is supposed to help you is two-faced: one side helps you recover, but the other disputes the legitimacy of your wounds. You're in the confluence of politics and budgeting, but you must stay the course or lose your benefits. One side desires your rehabilitation, but healing will lead to fiscal punishment and abandonment.

Social media occupies your time, and you learn about countless nonprofits that want to help. You attend meetings at service organizations where you find military politics alive and well. You go on several retreats with charities whose workers pamper and treat you honorably. You participate in several therapy sessions, but something is missing. You're going through the motions and things appear to be normal, but they're not. Nightmares continue, skepticism and indifferences hinder friendships, and memories interfere with intimacy. You turn to porn, drugs, alcohol, and risky activities. You yearn to join your comrades in Valhalla and anxiously await death. You pray for it, but God doesn't appease. *Of course He doesn't answer. He never does*, or so you think.

A new friend request pops up as you're fulfilling your indulgences of negative media. You accept the friendship and discover a unique ministry. He talks about a new norm, post-traumatic growth, and purpose. His transparency appears to be genuine. You discreetly follow him and discover that he, like many others, is working through the same storm as you. His threads talk about hope and happiness. He posts about adventures and drives home the ever-present absence of programs for spiritual wellness and family restoration. The two things that are most important to you are neglected by those who claim to care the most. You're inspired by his Christian faith and decide to attend a church in your area. But the church you attend is like the service organizations—political. You find a different church nearby that is hopping and fun. People are friendly, but they close you out of their circles. You gain respect for the pastor and seek his counseling, but all he can do is quote scripture. You finally decide to connect with the friend who seems to have it all together.

During a conversation with this friend, you discover a radical approach to Christianity. He tells you that the organization he's involved in is a church for warriors by warriors, that religious segregation is a thing of the past, and that Jesus had no thresholds. As you get involved with the program, you learn to focus on what you can do, not what you can't. You find purpose in serving. The long-lost pleasures that were buried deep in your childhood are reignited. Joy begins to overcome anger, and you make amends with your loved one. You attend a Survival Revival; spend time renewing your mind, body, and soul in the wilderness; and remember how bad life can really be. You return home with a revived warrior ethos and a renewed sense of purpose, meaning, and reason. You are now living in the new norm, adjusted, and refocused. You are no longer enslaved to ineffective programs, to the welfare state of entitlements, or to the spiritual virus. You're reborn.

Relapse

Excitement takes hold after discovering your new norm. There is freedom in living righteously. Your involvement with the Christian Adventure Network has led to the acceptance of Jesus as your Lord and Savior. You're sorrowful about the horrible things you've done in the past, are morally convicted of sinful behavior, and feel refreshed in your relationship with God. Things are going well, and the walls are coming down. You're plugged in at your local church, and their politics and cliques no longer bother you. You don't attempt to manipulate what the preacher says. Your relationship at home is extraordinarily better than it has ever been. You're involved, purposeful, and exploding with joy. But you receive a letter in the mail that informs you of a reduction in rating. They claim that you're better and no longer require as much financial support as you're receiving. Almost instantaneously, you hit a wall. All that buried anger, anxiety, frustration, and rage rear their ugly heads. Suicide, once again, reveals itself as an option. You fall apart in tears and pray for guidance, but silence owns the response.

This letter is a trigger of abandonment, attack, and instability. The one organization that must take care of you has counted you too costly to carry. This economic initiative is an attack on your well-being, your purpose, and your life, or so it appears. You curse them and forge a plan of reprisal. You get so caught up in this counterattack that you begin to neglect other life elements. You lose sleep, create distance with loved ones, and abandon friends. You're in a full-scale relapse. They unknowingly instigated a spiritual battle and left you for dead. Your friends and family evacuate from your path of destruction. They give way for the hurricane-like annihilation that lays in your wake. You're angry at everyone; even the guy who showed you the light seems distant. But solitude is one of the enemy's greatest weapons.

Spiritual battles can negatively impact mental health. Poor mental health slows cognitive ability and directly affects physical health. Your head is throbbing as if the TBI is fresh. Your joints swell, and chronic pain overtakes you. You're at a loss and not sure where the light is anymore. You recall the spiritual combat training you received. You don't want to hear psychobabble or explain your feelings. You need a battlefield to fight your war, a place that equips you for the struggle. You need a haven and a battle buddy who gets in the trenches with you.

You decide to reach out, and a rapid response team connects with you. They ask a couple of intrusive questions about your childhood and offer a battle plan to match. You're indifferent because you have so much going on. You cannot afford to commit any time, but you can't afford not to. Everything leads up to this decision: do I embellish my comfort zone and stay home, or do I go to war? Questions flood your mind, and you decide to warrior up.

Revival

The word *revival* often stimulates thoughts of old-school church, where a whole lot of preaching and praying goes on. This is for good reason: *revival* is a word mostly used to describe a religious outreach for the restoration of morality. Churches host evangelists from all around the world to ignite a spiritual fire in their communities. Revivals unite people for Christ, but many returns to their ways.

There was a time in history when people were hungry for the gospel.

Nowadays, however, many have become so distracted with technology and social media that they cannot even sit through a movie without using their devices. Our desire for thought-occupation and pseudo-busyness has left little room for imagination, conversation, and realization, much less faith. We're in perilous times that hinder commitment and spiritual endurance. We can only afford a few hours a week for God. This hyperdrive of intellect has slowly drained our faith banks, and now we're flatlined. We need an individualized revival to reinstate our motivation for a purpose-driven life, a life worthy of our Creator's imagination when He made us.

The Christian Adventure Network created a Survival Revival as a fitted modality for specific backgrounds. Its premise is to revive the warrior ethos. It is a wilderness expedition that purges outside distractions, purifies the soul, and empowers the warrior for spiritual battle. It's risky, removes luxuries, is uncomfortable, and can be frustrating. It draws out demons and is often physically painful. The Survival Revival is a spiritual furnace not advisable for those who find comfort in self-indulged pity parties. It is only for those who genuinely want to transfigure from battle born to born again.

A relapse can convince you that you're obsolete and that nobody cares. That is far from the truth. This wicked trickery is the enemy's recruiting strategy. Its' farce propaganda has defeated many warriors before you. Learn from their failures and our triumphs. Be as wise as a serpent but as harmless as a dove (Matthew 10:16). Many current rehabilitation and treatment models for PTSD and suicide aren't working. It's time to flesh out your aggression, anger, and hostility. It's time to locate a new target and take ownership of your life. Isaiah 43:19 demonstrates God's ability to renew our minds and souls through the wilderness, but it's up to you to take the journey.

Revivals aren't just spiritual; they instigate the essence of self-reliance that's within. Maybe you need a "ratatouille moment." Rekindling childhood memories that bring you joy is a defense tactic against negative memories. Use the five senses to combat PTS, STS, and VC. In these moments, when woodworking brings you back to your childhood through a smell, homemade ice cream lifts your smile through taste, and chirping birds tickle your soul, are the ingredients to formulate your cure. Are you ready for restoration, or are you comfortably complacent? Maybe it's time for you to pull the trigger and zero in. After all, being born again through battle is your living testimony.

7

ZERO IN

G rowing up around guns taught me respect for life, critical decision-making skills, and utmost safety. My shooting experience began with a Daisy BB gun. At first, hitting a can at ten feet away was difficult, but I was only seven years old. After a few hundred rounds, I began hitting the can at fifty feet. It was time to convert my gun into a weapon. My family and I knew poverty well, so I used this tool for hunting down sustenance. We ate everything I killed. I even shot a cottontail rabbit at thirty feet away while it was running from a dog. One shot, one kill—precision was my drill.

Joining the military was a natural choice. I was part of the 80 percent of military children who follow in their parent's footsteps. During basic military training, I observed countless peers who didn't have previous firearm experience. Their dependent childhood put them at a disadvantage. I scored forty-eight out of fifty shots and certified as a marksman. Later in my career, I was trained on sidearms. Once again, I scored high enough to make marksman.

After leaving the military, I received an invitation to hunt with Eddy Corona at Outdoor Experience 4 All (OE4A). They found a Rocky Mountain ram 750 yards away, across a deep valley, on the side of a mountain. We were looking into the sunset with a rising wind. My team consisted of a spotter (Ty Hart), a handler, and a wind/range coordinator. A single shot from the .338 sealed the ram's fate. Years of training led to this moment of precision, but it was truly my team that made it happen.

I received a second invitation, this time to hunt Coues whitetail in Southern Arizona. It's quite fulfilling to sit on the side of a mountain fellowshipping with a buddy while looking for the "Grey Ghost." Five years of pursuing this deer unsuccessfully had me feeling defeated, but this opportunity was a chance for redemption. I was blessed to hunt with my new friend Sam Hiatt. We both had tags, so I had to be on my game. We sat on a knoll facing the east side of a mountain with the sun rising at our backs. I spotted movement on the saddle of the hill, and Sam verified it was a buck with his binoculars. I was towing a 6.5 Creedmoor, but it wasn't my weapon. Getting in some pre-hunt practice was impossible due to logistics, and the owner wasn't there to adjust for the 530-yard shot. Sam was carrying a 300 Win Mag outfitted with a top-of-the-line scope. He said, "Mine will make that shot," so we eased back to a ledge for an uphill shot. It was tough to locate the buck through the scope, and when I did, he was behind a sequoia cactus. The only shot I had was when he stepped between the cactus arms. I slowly squeezed the trigger, and the recoil of the shot rocked me. Sam burst with excitement, "You got him!"

Those who practice life get better at living. When it appears people have it easy, consider the possibility that they've had plenty of practice. Most who have been around shooting sports, the military, or law enforcement know that practice makes perfect. Very few newbies step onto a range zeroed in. This anomaly does happen, but it's rare.

Comparing ourselves to others will hinder our accuracy unless that's what drives us. There is a higher chance that they've gone through something that has strengthened their resilience. We see the product of hardship, struggle, and perseverance. Those who practice will get better, and those who don't will surely fail.

The goal of a marksman is to hit the target. In our hidden war, spiritual combat training takes us to the shooting range. This range will intensify with skill progression. You may eventually find yourself in special ops through advanced training. However, we should never forget that the basics of zeroing in begin with locating the target.

On Target

Most shooters start at close range. Even after bore-sighting, experienced shooters start up close with a three-shot sequence before adjusting. Hitting anywhere on the target is a "tell" to adjust for zero (the bull's-eye). Experts debate the many strategies for zeroing in. Some get hung up on the technicalities and lose sight of the why. *How* isn't as important as *why*. Your why will bring you back to the range to practice countless hours until you finally achieve your *what*. *What* defines your *who* because what you do in life becomes who you are. *Who* is a conjecture of how you move forward. Who you are is how people will respond to what you do.

A bum on the side of the road stimulates strong feelings in most of us. We're either emotionally sympathetic or callously skeptic. A person in uniform elicits respect or rebellion. A preacher draws people in or pushes them away. How you determine your *who* will determine where you'll be. Where you end up in life isn't always up to you, though. We strive to control our fate, but divine intervention can create pivot points, as can our lifestyle choices. A series of bad decisions often leads to poverty or imprisonment. It's easy to blame others for where you're at, difficult to own it, and seemingly impossible to alter course. But there's hope in knowledge.

Acknowledging that sighting in a rifle requires up-close, hands-on tactics can help you sight in on life. Unexperienced shooters often pull their guns out of the manufacturer's box, load a round, and send one downrange in false confidence that they will hit the target without practice. A physicist with knowledge of ballistics but no experience behind the gun remains an amateur at the range. So goes life. Your traumatic experience can foster enlightenment but blaming others will lead to impoverished wellness. Your situation is like shooting a hole through the paper target at the range. You're on target, but you need more practice. Use experiences as opportunities to adjust your life - like getting a new firearm. Now, head back to the shooting bench and load another round.

Take Aim

Before the laser boresight, many shooters would expend round after round trying to zero in. Up until now, some have been doing the same thing at life—aimlessly sending shots down range in hopes of hitting the target. Recognize that without knowing where your rounds are hitting, you can't make proper adjustments. Closing the distance is imperative. Now that you're up close and personal, take aim. A steady hold and smooth trigger pull can land your bullet in the exact place you're holding over (not considering ballistic rise and fall, wind, elevation, earth curvature, etc.). You're on the shooting bench with a stable hold. Slow your breathing, aim, and slowly squeeze the trigger. *Bang!* You're on paper. Now's not the time to adjust, though. Most shooters send three rounds downrange to account for flinching, jumping the shot, or any other anomaly that alters shooter precision.

Three rounds going through the same hole is consistency. If they go anywhere else, you're inconsistent, something is wrong with your gun and scope setup, or your gun and ammo don't match. Let's consider, just for a moment, that you put all three rounds through the same hole. You adjust and send three more downrange, zeroed in on the bull's-eye. It's time to move your target out to the next level. The farther away it is, the less room you have for error. You shoot several times at different ranges and are now zeroed in and ready for long-range shooting. Here's where things get tricky because more people are involved.

You aspire to be an impact agent, to build bridges, to shine the light of hope. The tragedy in your life is now a positive influence. Your experience, adjustments, and practice have made you a marksman. Precision is everything. Locate the target and discover your purpose. Aim with intention. Now choose the right moment to pull the trigger.

Trigger Pull

Each style of shooting requires different trigger-pull procedures. Snatching or slapping the trigger only works for shotguns as they cover more substantial portions of the target. They are traditionally used to hit moving marks, such as birds, rabbits, and squirrels. The rapid-pull technique is for semiautomatic firearms but isn't precise. This technique is also known as rapid fire, cover fire, or suppressive fire. Aggressively pulling the trigger as fast as you can sends a lot of bullets downrange quickly, but's it's more of a "spray and pray" technique. Then there's the slow, steady squeeze used for long-range precision shooting. Big-game hunters, snipers, and sharpshooters use this method to place a round on the exact spot they desire. Each type of shooting requires different styles of trigger pull, as does every decision.

Decisions aren't always life-altering, so don't overthink them all. Some choices require snatching the trigger because the opportunity may quickly pass. Other decisions, such as leading a diverse team of disaster-response personnel, require the rapid-fire technique. Big decisions that could alter the course of your life require precision. You must understand the concept of paralysis by analysis. This barrier arises all the time, and people miss out. But in contrast, using the wrong decision-making strategy can create havoc in your life.

Triggers have guards because accidental discharges occur if you don't protect against them. Learning the art of pulling the trigger on decisions isn't the same as "being triggered," but it isn't much different. We get triggered because we lack trigger guards. Before guards were invented, more people were accidentally shooting themselves in the foot. We have come a long way since accidental discharges. Today, we consider such an accident to be the result of negligence because all safety measures are in place to avoid firearm mishaps.

Relatively speaking, your actions occur because you decide to pull the trigger, or you fail to protect yourself. You are your weapon, and it is your responsibility to develop a guard. Overcome accidental discharges by identifying your triggers. Spend time on the range getting zeroed in by practicing appropriate trigger pulls. Find your why in life, and you'll discover purpose. Finally, follow through because people who are untrue to their word are repulsive.

Follow Through

Your word matters. It separates friend from foe, fake from real, glory from demise. Loyalty, honor, and integrity define who you are. Respect, courtesy, and love reflect what you are. This behavior is the ammunition that you load into your chamber. What you do with your life and how you do it is synonymous. Everyone's life is different though. We have examples to follow, like Dr. Martin Luther King Jr., who led the revolution of equal rights, and President Abraham Lincoln, who spearheaded the abolishment of slavery. These are men who stood in the face of resistance, traveling unknown paths against the grain of normalcy. We live in their shadows of achievement, hoping for an opportunity to leave our mark. We explore pathways for innovative change but measure up to the world's standards instead of our own. Rather than following positive examples, we often fold in the struggle. The path of righteousness requires intestinal fortitude. It requires us to follow through.

Sharpshooters know that trigger pull is irrelevant if there's no follow-through. Any movement of the gun can alter the trajectory of the bullet. We often exaggerate follow-through by staying behind the scope for a few seconds after the shot. This procedure ensures that we remain on target. There is only one path to freedom from suicide, PTS, and other spiritual health issues, but it's obstructed by measurable outcomes, cultural stipulations, political correctness, and even our cohorts. These obstructions aren't always counterproductive, though. We amuse ourselves by trying to define success. Success, however, is infinitely defined by the result. If our means don't justify the ends, then our lives are being lived in vain. We are unworthy in His image, but we can be worthy in our own accord.

Slaves were not freed by their own hand but on the shoulders of President Lincoln and likeminded patriots. Freedom was a small step precluded by segregation. Dr. King picked up President Lincoln's mission for equality and aided in its follow-through. King stepped into Lincoln's purpose to get it on target. He zeroed in on the objective and slowly squeezed the trigger. Likewise, Jesus taught us to love. It is up to us to stand in His image and follow through on His purpose. For me, that is the abolishment of denominational segregation. There is Christ; then there's religion. I've taken several shots. I'm on paper, I'm adjusted, and now it's time to reload and send another one downrange. Dear Church, will you respond?

Reload

We've homed in on decision-making strategies by defining the three trigger-pull techniques. We're trained on steady hold and follow-through. We have our target in site, understand the concept of aiming, and are zeroed in on the bull's-eye. We've taken our shot, and now it's time to reload and shoot again.

Marksmen expend countless rounds of ammunition refining accuracy, which leads to precision. Making decisions is no different. If we get hung up on a wrong choice and never take another shot, we can never move forward. We'll lose friends, family, and cohorts, but we must never lose hope. Hope is the essence of light, established by opportunity, and granted by self-endurance. Hope cannot belong to someone who doesn't seek it, just like marksmanship comes at the expense of countless hours of practice. Load another round and take another shot—if not for yourself, then for someone you love.

If you're like me, then the thought of death doesn't paralyze you. Life, however, is so incumbent that I once feared the destructive force of my existence. Had I died in combat; I would be a hero in my children's eyes. But because I lived and carry the burdens of war with me, I've made some behavioral choices that didn't demonstrate unconditional love. Some of my shots drove a wedge in my relationships, and it broke my heart. I'm well educated on all coping mechanisms in existence but often yearn for self-punishment instead.

Zeroing in doesn't mean you always hit the target. Sometimes a gust of wind, a bug in your ear, or an anomaly impacts the precision of your shot. Remember, you can always recover by loading another round and sending it downrange. But if you quit pulling the trigger, if you tap out, if you commit suicide—you're done. You'll not have another chance. You'll never get better. Your wish to become a marksman will be lost and forgotten. Be the hero that you are, the warrior who stands in the face of fury. Zero in on your life's mission and take your shot.

8

TIMELESS TIMING

The launch of a not-for-profit organization that saves heroes, raises the next generation of warriors, and restores families came at the right moment in time. The suffering I bore created a better understanding of the need. Though my efforts have influenced countless other initiatives, it is the divine Spirit of God that deserves the credit. His master plan and timing link us together. This opportunity is the bridge between light and dark, the connection to spiritual strength and fortitude. We labor in vain unless we focus on the eternal product of everlasting life.

There are few people creating positive social change by bridging the gap between warriors and the Church. Most church leaders are indifferent to outside ministries because they want to protect their "flock". Skepticism exists because of theology. Like citizens who fear warriors due to a lack of understanding, most churches have ignored my plea to partner. This baffles me because all I want to do is get more warriors in their pew. Imagine the impact a church can have if they empowered mission-driven warriors for Christ.

Many organizations refrain from religious associations in fear of exclusion. There are few ministries based solely on love, grace, mercy, accountability, and forgiveness. Most are indoctrinated with religious beliefs. This isn't all bad, but it does foster segregation. Unfortunately, a lot of churches have become like our government—active with rules and regulations but lacking Christ-like character. Character is the product of a warrior's experience in the furnace and is the fountain of salvation. We appall our government's factious conformity to minority influence because a democratic republic is supposed to function on majority rule. Warriors want our dog in the fight, and to us, timing is relevantly irrelevant.

Have you ever heard the phrase "timing is everything"? In a productive conversation, your words must be sewn together strategically to make a point or used to navigate a discussion in an intentional direction. Throwing words around without consideration of others is like bringing Christmas presents to Thanksgiving: it works, but it's not fitting. The same rules apply for our actions, for our careers, and God's call on our life.

Moses didn't rise to his purpose until he was eighty years old (Exodus 7:7). He spent forty years learning, forty years in grooming, and forty years leading ex-slaves around the wilderness (Deuteronomy 34:7). Eighty years of prep work is unacceptable in our culture today. Many refer to people in this age group as elders, old-timers, or in the worst case, burdens. But that which our culture considers a liability, God deems valuable.

We're caught up on instant gratification and immediate results. We live by goals, plans, and visions of our design but get distressed when things don't go according to plan. When we fail to meet our goals, we fall into a depressed state of mind. When our vision falters, we desperately grasp for the next big thing. But instead of panicking when redirection occurs, we should wait for an opening, a call, an opportunity. Being bogged down in the daily grind to justify our existence hinders our celestial purpose. Doing nothing while waiting is worse because we're not growing or earning our keep. Moses was called to return to his beginning, to his roots. This hard reset is where we find redemption.

In the Beginning

Let's rewind to what was - instead of what could've been. Reminiscing about the good ol' days gives us footing in the now. Many had a childhood that they'd rather not visit. A mental health specialist may recommend that you work on this area of your life. If you have a professional to walk through it with you, then fight those demons. But if you are all alone in reading this book, then I suggest you don't. Instead, let's dig up good memories and refresh our minds and spirits. The beginning holds evidence on who we are as individuals. It is the start line for life's obstacle course.

Everyone's walk is different, from the beginning until now. Only you can carry the weight of your journey.

What do you remember from your childhood that stimulates good memories? Is it the smell of your father's woodworking shop, your grandparents' smokehouse, or peach cobbler sitting in the windowsill? Maybe it's the taste of apple cider on Thanksgiving, muscadine grapes from the farmer's vineyard, or cotton candy at the fair. Can you remember the feel of sand between your toes, the warmth of a campfire on a cold day, or the gentle breeze of a hot summer night? Look deeply. Do you recall star gazing, discovering art in the clouds, or fireflies dancing in the night? Maybe it's the sound of cracking twigs as a deer approached your stand, the forest coming to life as dawn welcomed the day, or the whip-poor-will stoically charming the night.

The five senses (touch, taste, smell, hearing, and sight) deposit memories for a lifetime. Most of these senses are nurtured through nature. Rarely do I receive feedback from urban-raised individuals about their childhood memories originating from inner-city living. Most memories are from outdoor experiences. But what happens when an injury causes you to lose those precious memories or if you never collected them? Has God really let you down, or is He setting you up to be like Moses?

God created earth as we know it from a formless and dark void by merely speaking it into existence (Genesis 1:1–31). You may be an evolutionist or just don't care, and that's okay. One cannot argue, however, that light lacks dominion over darkness. It is impossible and therefore void of theoretical value. If sin is darkness and righteousness is light, then why do we allow the darkness within to triumph over the light?

We indulge our incompetency with strife and struggle to master ourselves all on our own. We hold the power of light but decline to use it. We refuse to acknowledge that this spiritual flashlight is the Word of God—the Bible. "In the beginning was the Word, and the Word was with God, and the Word was God" (John 1:1).

Many have witnessed abuse, manipulation, and neglect of the light to propagate personal agendas. This atrocity happens way too often, but I refuse to allow my relationship with one person to become affected by another. It is our responsibility to manage the light and to use it appropriately. Shining it in people's faces will blind them, so light up the path instead.

In any given moment, an opportunity for rebirth is present. Planting and growing Christ in someone will allow them to be a new creation. Their old habits pass away, and they are renewed (2 Corinthians 5:17). This resurrection is not forcible, and the timing must be exact. We are each on an individual journey. Like Moses, we can become magnificently purposeful, but we often must go through training and tribulations to get there.

Maybe you think that your moment has slipped away, or perhaps you got impatient and launched prematurely. Even those who achieve greatness have doubts. The fork in the road challenges us with decisiveness. Interstate travel is destination driven, not moment driven. If you take the wrong turn or miss your exit, your timing gets manipulated, but you can always turn around. Rest assured that we are never too far gone for a divine purpose. Our beginnings may simply need a hard reset. Don't fret. The path you're returning from wasn't taken in vain.

Hard Reset

The most sophisticated technologies are often repairable in the simplest ways. Step one: unplug said device. Step two: wait. Step three: plug it back in. Many times, it's that simple. Nearly every great leader we read about understands the value of unplugging. Even Jesus disconnected countless times throughout His short life span. According to SoulsShepherding. org (2019), Jesus retreated twenty-three times throughout his estimated three years of ministry. He valued an intimate relationship with God and cultivated that bond in nature. His sabbaticals weren't full of occupying tasks, travel, or indoor luxuries. He used the great outdoors for personal revivals and to reset. Earlier, I implicated retreating as a form of defeat. Now you discover how much value I place on it. You may need to unplug if you're caught up on the fine details of statistics, if you're self-imprisoned, or if you're task saturated.

Before exhaustion, failure, or a rash decision that will end it all, retreat. Many psychologists and medical professionals would have you believe that being alone is dangerous, and they are correct. Being at war with an overwhelming occupying force can seem hopeless. As previously described, you need a team of special operators to ward off the enemy. But this won't rectify the situation. Remember, your first step is to unplug. Get away from what is bringing you down (person, place, or thing). Cease daily operations until you're squared away. Next, wait.

Typically, we wait less than a minute for a piece of technology to reset, but you may require a longer delay. The design of my Survival Revival does just that. It's the hard reset that gets you plugged back in and back online as a functioning member of your family and community. Patience is vital when we strive for God's intervention, timing, or touch. You are irreplaceable; technology is not. You are much more complex than technology, riddled with intricate details that are unique to you. But everyone's hard reset is the same. You must be alone with your Creator, with no outside distractions, fleshing out deviant thoughts for Him to devour. This is your moment, your pivot point. Discover His timing on your life and be renewed in mind, body, and spirit.

Pivot Point

Wasting time is one of my greatest pet peeves. Turning around a vehicle after five minutes on the road because someone forgot something at home is stressful for me, much less restarting life after thirteen years of military service. Doing things in vain is a waste of time. Proving myself to civilians is done in vain because they're quick to dismiss me after even the slightest mistake. "Street credit" is as fragile as the stock market and fluctuates with social trends.

In uniformed services, credibility is sewn on the sleeve, pinned on the collar, displayed on the chest, or hung around the neck. The Medal of Honor, for example, is recognized anywhere in the world by military personnel and induces a salute. A Purple Heart recognizes warriors who were wounded in combat. It symbolizes a price paid for freedom, a sacrifice of physical proportion. Rank is displayed on the collar or sleeve to indicate leadership. The rank and file organize the command structure. Respect of position is automatic, but for the person wearing the uniform, it is earned.

Once earned, these forms of credibility are tough to dismiss. Civilians put little value in people's word, much less their history. Who are you now and what have you done for me lately, is a more common theme. Many squander time on petty things, such as chasing fame or fortune, being hypersensitive (easily offended), or pondering change without provocation. The most extreme case of time negligence is living in the *when* instead of the *now*. Your past is gone, and your future is yet to be. Your now is who you are, not who you were or who you'll be. Each day we earn our keep, grinding forward to make ends meet. The end of yesterday is the beginning of today, and the end of today will be the start of tomorrow. There's nothing we can do to alter yesterday while we're in this moment. Lessons are learned from our past and applied to our future. Plans set us up for success, but we're not there—we're here. Time is wasted when we don't see that, when we don't nurture our direct environments. Each noun that you're currently around is the most valuable thing you have in this moment. This epiphany was a difficult lesson for me to accept. What I considered a waste of time was actually my inability to discern the value of my immediate surroundings.

Vainly sowing into ungrateful people is discouraging. Like weeds that choke out the seeds you plant, the soil being unfertile, or the ground is too shallow (Matthew 13:1–58). This discouragement can pollute our spirits with a "waste of time" mentality. But 2 Corinthians 9:6 says that our investment in people will result in the product of our own making. It's okay to sow bountifully, casting seeds broadly, but know that only the seeds that drop on cultivated land will bring forth fruit.

Preparing the land is just as important as planting. Someone must plow the ground, pull the weeds, and remove the stones. It's dirty work and not socially appealing. There is no fame or fortune in it, and the world would have you believe that it's of little importance. This work is not measurable by our hands and therefore has few investors. Churches count saved souls through the efforts of those in the fields toiling through blood, sweat, and tears so that the land is ready for the Maker. Sometimes, however, there are too many roots or a boulder in the way. Testing the ground is an essential first step to determine if it's suitable for growing, but many of us dive in without hesitation.

Our paths often intersect with others who have shared experiences. Sometimes we travel the wrong way and must turn around. That's our pivot point! Turning around allows us to return to the right path for our lives and use our experiences to help others. Your time astray is either wasteful or productive. The difference is where you stand when considering this. Those suffering from suicidal ideations, PTS, depression, or anxiety get stuck on their pivot points. Cognitively, they understand that there is freedom from this burden, but every time they near the surface they're pulled back down. Without a team on the outside to lift them up, they drown in self-propagated demise. Pivot points are always up to us, but we often require help in finding the path to freedom.

Growing up in church makes it tough to nail down a specific date of salvation. For those who didn't have this luxury but came to know Jesus later in life, their transfiguration day is much clearer. My temptations were met with resiliency training. Proverbs 22:6 tells us that children raised righteously will strive for righteousness (at some point in their lives). What about those who were never gifted morality as a child, whose parents' vulgar lifestyles sabotaged their childhood? That foundation can either impede or promote difference, but the choice is yours.

The right path can make you feel like you're heading to Mount Everest. The wrong way can appear like a white sandy beach with Hollywood models in dainty swimsuits. Who in their right mind would choose a path of resistance and hazard over luxury and beach babes? I'll tell you—those with foresight.

Individuals who acknowledge fulfillment in overcoming obstacles take the road to Everest. The beach is full of self-indulged, disease-ridden, greedy, whoremongers who are delusional and destructive. A tidal wave is coming, and they'll never see it because of the distractions. Only a few conquer Mount Everest. In both circumstances, you cannot remain on top of the mountain or at the beach forever. There is always something or someone around the corner that is waiting for you. Whether you pivot or push forward, be ready for your moment.

Intersecting Paths

In 2011, before deploying to Afghanistan, a divine mission was placed on my heart. Called to use human curiosity as an opportunity, I developed a wallet ministry. My family and I lived in Tucson, Arizona, at the time, stationed at Davis-Monthan Air Force Base. We attended a large church there, where I served in the children's ministry. My spirit burned for evangelism—not the evangelism you see on television or inside church walls, but the missionary-style evangelism that's on the streets of America. I wanted to be the missionary who builds the Church flock for pastors to shepherd, a Christian warrior who scales the fortress walls to infiltrate enemy territory. It seems legit, right? Someone with a divine appointment to serve the King and promote church attendance should be every pastor's dream disciple, but it's not. The church's response to my vision was skeptical, and I felt rejected. My grit and love for Christ persevered, and we launched this ministry without assistance. We began by purchasing one thousand black wallets. I drafted a letter that read something like this:

> If you're reading this message, it means that you've found me for a reason. Your path to this place and time was predestined. Any deviation and we would have never met. You have purpose and meaning. This is your moment to become the person you were born to be. Our paths have intersected to give you an opportunity: either keep this wallet as a reminder of this moment or put me back in play. In either case, know that you are loved unconditionally by a Father who sacrificed His only Son for your freedom. God is waiting for you. Find a local church today and plug in.

We invested countless hours in folding letters and stuffing wallets. We distributed them broadly at gas stations, grocery stores, airports, and parks. Places that allowed God's intervention to work through what many views as coincidence. Although we own our paths, traveling and making decisions through free will, the Holy Spirit walks with us. God's presence is continually existent. He stands with us through thick and thin, highs and lows, wickedness and righteousness. He never abandons or forsakes us. He is the navigator in our flight deck, the protector of our command center. He is the good wolf that we should feed, our conscientious objections to sinful tolerance. He may be presently dormant, awaiting your call. Don't wait till you're about to sink; wake Him before the storm arrives. Get your plan intact. You reading this book didn't happen by coincidence. Instead, it's God speaking to you through me.

Never Too Late

The rejection I faced from the church wasn't an anomaly, and I tried not to take it personally. My decision to remain a parishioner there originated through a rebellious spirit. Many of us endure temptation to go against the grain. I turned my flaw into a fierce weapon against the enemy. Though it hurt to face division in the Kingdom, I would not allow it to drive a wedge between Jesus and me. Thousands, if not millions of followers, have left the Church because of indifference. They have submitted to the enemy and abandoned assembling with other believers. There is a saying, "You cannot make it to heaven on someone's shirttail," but I add that you sure can make it to hell under someone's heel. Having a bad meal at a restaurant doesn't stop you from eating out, so don't allow a bad experience at a church stop you from going again.

Allowing someone to interfere with your relationship with God demonstrates immaturity in spirit. There's nothing wrong with changing churches, but to remain absent and linger in solitude is to instigate spiritual demise. It feeds spiritual infection that hungers for your soul, for self-destruction. Nearly every church I have attended in my life (more than fifty due to countless moves in the military) had issues. Some were theologically flawed, while others were off the rails. Large churches are often indifferent to extending ministry opportunities to parishioners who don't hold leadership positions within the church. Leaning on my own understanding created a wedge. However, I found redemption when I learned to trust God's plan and to trust in Him.

If I have described you and you're offended, then consider the possibility that humility comes at a cost. That cost, however, has already been paid. It isn't too late to return. You are not too far gone. This may very well be the revelation that provides you the insight and courage to join team Jesus. Don't fret when you face rejection—grow. Don't entertain skepticism—flow. Don't empower the Devil—go.

Refusing to get back into the fight. It is nearly impossible to have a stable relationship with God and remain absent from the church. If this is you, then deep dive into your conscience and explore your emotional core and your spiritual state. Assuming self-righteousness is your first sign. Test your reason for not attending church and see if it aligns with the whole Bible, not just a particular verse. Otherwise, you may discover regret in your life that was avoidable.

Forecasting Regret

If you knew about future regrets, wouldn't you try to change things? Most of us would alter course to reduce the possibility of remorse. Putting self-interest aside allows freedom from imminent burdens. The saying "I wish I would've known then what I know now" is dense with laden thought. It stems from regret and manufactures twenty-twenty hindsight. This book holds the solution: it provides twenty-twenty foresight. You are at the well, but it is up to you to drink.

Accurately predicting the future is impossible. However, researchers can make educated guesses about the future based on current activities. For example, homosexual intercourse is damaging and unnatural; drugs are a catalyst for crime, death, and destruction; and irresponsible consumption causes poor health and obesity. The decisions we make now can lead to regret later. I'm not here to bash your choices or to cast judgment. Only Jesus is qualified to do so. Instead, I'm merely attempting to demonstrate how you can intercept future regrets. This section isn't focused on sinful behavior, but rather on lukewarm lifestyles. This information is unknown to most until they are gray haired and flirting with death. Two life elements that we most often take for granted, that we ponder at the end of our road, are faith and family.

In my studies of greatest regrets, the two most common concerns men had on their deathbeds were faith and family. Over 80 percent wished they had spent more time with their families, and nearly 70 percent regretted not doing more for the Kingdom. The 80 percent was generated by random sampling, whereas the 70 percent focused on individuals who claimed salvation. These findings led me to study the roughly 20 percent of people who are getting it right. Men and women who have balanced lives and are free from spiritual infection are the supreme examples for us to follow.

We often get caught up in following famous individuals who are unbalanced and sometimes commit suicide. We chase fame and fortune because we think we desire power and authority, while in reality, we simply need to know that our lives mean something. My friends, you can only find this in faith and family. Nothing else can satisfy this craving, but we continue to go astray. Generation after generation wallow in regretful behavior. The code for overcoming the derailment of your purpose is within the core of your spirit. Your uniqueness does not exempt you from a conclusive ending. Only your ability to overcome a desire for personal gain can add quality to your time here on earth. After all, your timing means nothing if not aligned with a divine appointment.

9

THE RISE AND FALL
OF A WARRIOR

This book was composed to provide spiritual empowerment for the warrior who once was, who is, and who is to come. It's a solution for the mental health crisis our world is in. The rebirth of our heroes through battle is such a unique experience that most churches cannot handle it (yet). This gap pushes warriors into isolation. We are treated as black sheep even though we are sheepdogs, spiritually fortified through combat. The rise of a warrior begins in their childhood, but so does their fall. The seed of success and failure takes root during adolescent years. These roots deepen after a traumatic experience, leading to a fruitful or a disease-stricken system (akin to a fruit tree).

A hero is birthed in the extramundane. The Creator strikes a spark that ignites the warrior ethos. Childhood grooms us for battle. Some lives end tragically, while others continue into posterity. The worst possibility isn't necessarily having life cut short but instead creating a path of destruction that leads to suicide. It is difficult to remember warriors for who they were when they become so ruinous.

To the fatigued warrior who's reading this, know that there's hope for you yet. Your outlandish behavior may have cost you friends and family, but it doesn't have to cost your soul. You rose to the occasion in defense of our great nation; now rise to fight for yourself. Pull up on the controls, pump the brakes, hold fast, or do whatever's necessary to survive this battle. You are at war, plagued by a virus that's eating away at your foundation. It isn't you but the enemy that encamps within. It's time for an antibiotic to build your immunity against foreign spirits and to rise again. Not everyone will respond equally because our roots are different. Some of us want the shortcut, while others would rather play the long game. Stay the course and finish strong.

Shortcuts

Do you prefer the destination over the journey? Is your desired productiveness constrained by time? This impatience is a shortcut to obversion. Apply KISS to the process and cross a bridge that leads to greener pastures. First, we must recognize the error of our ways. We cannot get stronger unless we practice overcoming weaknesses, which we must first identify. This cannot happen unless we confess our shortcomings. Next, repent and be serious about changing. Achieving righteousness is impossible but striving for virtue is attainable. Nobody, absolutely nobody, is perfect (outside of Jesus). Therefore, we lack the qualification to judge one another. However, we must sharpen each other to strive for perfection and build one another up when we fail. There's power in positive reinforcement. Last, pray. While praying should always be the first thing to consider, purposeful prayers occur in this three-step process. Otherwise, we may very well be praying aimlessly.

If you've completed the first two steps and are ready to dive into prayer, then here's an example to follow:

> God, I submit myself to you. I confess my sins, knowing and unknowing, and ask for your help in removing them from me. Wash me clean, forgive me, and help me forgive myself. Allow me an opportunity to make amends, to restore relationships, and to be redeemed through the blood of your Son. I believe in the death and resurrection of Jesus Christ, the Holy Spirit that strengthens and encourages me, and your purpose in my life. Fight this war for me or join me on the battlefield. In the name of Jesus, I evict the enemy and claim victory over that which

held me captive. Fill me with your spring of life, overflow my cup with grace and mercy, allow me to love and be compassionate. Surround me with positive people and grant me purpose. My life is yours; I surrender it. Restore my soul, ignite my fire, and put me back in play—but in your time, Lord, not mine. May your light shine through me that others may be blessed. Give me the courage and wisdom to serve you. Let your will be done and free me from the burden of my own. Amen.

These three steps will help you get back on the horse, but it takes humility and knowledge. To do this, you must be ready to change for the better. If you are caught in the cat-and-mouse game for benefits, then you may not be ready. In that case, I suggest you play the long game. Either way, the only productive move is to press forward.

Some would suggest that a shortcut is a quick fix that doesn't last, and they would be right in most cases. The above three-step process is the only exception. Shortcuts are known for getting people lost, being dangerous, and discounting the hard work that goes into development. Shortcuts, when on target, can be ideal. However, life takes practice, and practice happens over time with experiences. Courage and resilience fortify the long game, but what if you can't see the end?

The Long Game

Although most of us desire a quick fix, many unknowingly make the long road turn. We attempt to overcome brokenness through cultural solutions. We linger in worldly pleasures until they lose their allure. We go deeper into the rabbit hole, trying to discover new pathways to numb our pain, fill our emptiness, and satisfy cravings. We pride ourselves in our works and good deeds, count our successes, and build our careers. Time is spent like money, but unlike time, money is replaceable. Personal conquests lead to an abyss of hopelessness, a deep dark hole that is all-consuming. The world convinces us that happiness and peace can be earned, when in fact they are gifts that many refuses to accept.

The shortcut previously described is a quick fix that draws you into a different type of long game. The world's long game is the pursuit of temporary happiness, but the divine long game pursues eternal pleasure. In this, our long game can be a shortcut to temporary joy, and the alternative is a long game for escaping the pits of hell. Let's take a minute to untangle this. I trust in the concept of KISS and don't want you to have to be a scholar to understand what I'm saying.

Shortcuts can be harmful if people don't fully understand their *why*. The long game is best if you have already taken the step of securing your salvation. Shortcuts can be good if you're not at your wit's end. The long game can be bad, though, if you don't believe. It boils down to your faith in the higher power that is called the Trinity. Without understanding the working process of the Trinity, we cannot fully grasp this solution.

God, the Father, is the creator of the long game but also sent His Son Jesus the Christ as a shortcut to Him. Jesus played the long game and was horrendously crucified to become our shortcut. He handed us off to the Holy Spirit, which dwells inside each of us. In the 1978 book *What Shall This Man Do?* Watchman Nee referred to it as "consciousness of life" (p. 150). While the Trinity is holistic, each element plays a different part. You may recognize the three elements of yourself—mind, body, and soul—the culmination of which is your functional spirit (personal perspective). Our spirits link these three elements with purpose. Additionally, they connect us to others.

In simple terms, if you're about to commit suicide, then take the shortcut. Force yourself to believe. Fake it until you make it because practicing anything will make you better at something. If you're already a believer, then play the long game. Enjoy life and refuse the haste of individual timing. You're allowed to fall as many times as necessary, but you're not allowed to stay down. Get back on your feet and do your part to survive, to escape, and to win your war.

Apply Pressure

Pressure can be applied in many ways. Paramedics compress wounds to stop bleeding; law enforcement officers squeeze criminals for confessions; and preachers convict to save souls. For a more common analogy, let's look at different levels of coaching. T-ball coaches are supposed to be patient and gentle, extending unlimited amounts of grace and mercy. For those of us at this level in faith, that's what we need. It's the forgiveness that draws us closer to the game, the nonjudgmental peers who befriend us, the vision of one day playing in the big leagues. But as we grow, we realize an increased level of pressure for excellence. High school coaches push their players hard and expect competitiveness. They hold their players more accountable and increase demand because they want to win and strive to draw out the best in each player, but some players quit. These players are loyal to themselves, not the team. They cannot handle the pressure, so they either switch sides or cease playing altogether. This baffles many coaches.

Coaches endure condemnation from fans, parental cursing, and even abandonment from the ones they coach. Such players have invested years of their lives getting to this level only to throw it all away. For the players who move forward into the Major Leagues, they realize that they've reached the top. Coaches at this level are primarily managers. Yes, these coaches do run drills and go through the motions, but their players should already be skilled athletes. Coaches at this level focus on team synergy. Training the team to function as one unit is vital to winning the World Series. This leadership is comparable to God with His elected representatives (preachers, ministers, evangelists, disciples, missionaries, etc.). Unfortunately, His reps aren't synergetic.

Their masterful skill-level produces professional-athlete-type arrogance. They are the best; they know the game and what to do. They made it to the big leagues, and now they lead the way for upcoming aspiring athletes. However, an indifference to working with others fosters segregation and division. We're not talking about something as inconsequential as baseball, though; we're talking about life or death. We're talking about war. Like a combat medic who applies pressure to stop the bleeding, the disciplinarian coach applies pressure to remove poor attitudes. Sometimes, though, demand isn't enough. One must take a radical step to stop the bleeding.

In my studies, I've come to realize that the Church is losing believers faster than it can gain them. This is symbolic of profuse bleeding from a spiritual wound that we must attend to. The Church does not track their losses. Records only reflect those they "save." But the Church is a significant element of your cure. Many of those suffering from mental health issues have lost faith in the Church. They have been outwitted by the enemy to believe perception as truth while, in fact, attitudes are only the reality of the beholder. Unifying perspectives by synergizing God's reps is how we cauterize this wound. We must humbly accept the coaching style at the level in which we play.

Surrender and Fight

The Church phrase, "surrender and fight" can seem to contradict the warrior ethos. Using these words in the same song insinuates an oxymoronic philosophy. However, after dealing with personal mental health issues and gaining knowledge on my cure, I've come to realize that this isn't hypocritical at all. As a matter of fact, it is the most accurate statement to ever exist regarding spiritual warfare. One cannot continue to fight a battle in solidarity. To do so breeds contention and disobedience. We must give God our troubles, for He is the Master of our fate, the Healer of our hurt, the Maker of our destiny. Fighting alone renders God obsolete and thus the spiritual antibiotic useless. Defeat is inevitable without reinforcements. You are surrounded by the enemy yet refuse to call in air support. Surrendering doesn't mean waving a white flag to the enemy; it means acknowledging your inability to fight the battle alone. Grant team members an opportunity to do their part and allow them to bless you.

In the television series *We Were Soldiers*, Easy Company was pinned down by the Germans. Lieutenant Spears approached Private Blithe, who was in fear for his life. This fear caused him to freeze up and not return fire at the enemy. The lieutenant said something that has resonated with me for quite some time (paraphrased): "Get up and fight like you're already dead because you will be if you don't." His actual words were, "You think that there's still hope, but, Blithe, the only hope you have is to accept the fact that you're already dead. And the sooner you accept that, the sooner you'll be able to function the way a soldier is supposed to function."

I died to myself when I surrendered my life to Christ. In so doing, I gained a new uniform, reinforced battle rattle, upgraded training, and a leadership team that makes sound decisions. Every one of my team members is invaluable, fearless, and gung ho. We have common ground in our inseparable, unbreakable bonds, and impenetrable armor. We are undefeatable.

Ascertaining such collaborative unity came at a cost, though. I had to give up myself and the sense that I am the owner of my brokenness. A burden that breaks the back of the most potent warriors is a weight I could no longer carry. In my weakness, I became strong. I am now more invincible than ever. My fight is won before I even show up, but God allows me to be involved anyway.

The Common Thread

We all face two common facts: life and death. You reading this means you're physically alive, and hopefully by this point you've become spiritually alive. Most spiritually dead people will not make it to this point because they allow a schism to create distraction or indifference. Seasoned professionals may arrive here because they understand the value of bridging knowledge, extracting specific details, and understanding the full list of ingredients in a formula. The invaluable data delivered in this book isn't of my own volition. I'd much rather be hunting or fishing, but I've accepted the terms of being a vessel for His revolutionary movement. Those who accept my findings share a common thread of divinity, which is the base of everyone's existence.

Law enforcement officers share a commonality in their fight against injustices. Firefighters stand together to extinguish destructive flames. Paramedics ponder possible life-saving strategies, while military personnel take the fight abroad. Teachers educate, truck drivers deliver, farmers feed, and so on. In every nook and cranny of society, there are common threads that bring us together. Denomination separation of the Church occurred because of humans' desire for camaraderie. Cliques and circles form because of mutual interests and cohesiveness. It's the natural order of humanity. But what if I told you that these common threads divide rather than unite us? All the lines, such as the thin blue line and red, green, white, and black lines, cause division. The rainbow, once a reminder of God's promise, is now used to identify the homosexual community.

Once upon a time, all Americans united under the Stars and Stripes. Today, however, this is reserved for patriotic people who believe in tradition.

To hold fast in defense of a personal thread is to guard against unity. The argument about whose life means what stems from a spirit of segregation. If we could recognize and distinguish that the only two threads that genuinely matter are good and evil, we could begin overcoming the internal battle that leads to suicide.

The origin of suicide isn't necessarily in mental health issues, though it's a leading cause. I theorize that mental health is the spiritual essence of our existence. These two go together; one cannot exist without the other. People with perfect mental health commit suicide, as do people with poor mental health. I discovered through divine influence that an imbalance in life leads to spiritual illness. This occurs well before signs and symptoms of mental health issues. To be diagnosed with PTSD, anxiety, or depression, one must have suffered continuous effects for a specified period. The common response of mental health providers is to prescribe medication, recommend alternative therapies, and talk. Few, if any, realize that the solution is a culmination of ten well-balanced life ingredients. Limited stock is invested in this holistic concept because many specialize in one or two of these life elements, not all ten.

A large amount of firsthand intel is applied to this book. From the brink of destruction rose a divine mission for other warrior families—10 CAN, Inc. On this journey, I bought in to the term *Hidden Hero*. Civilians who have never experienced what warriors go through and who believe them heroic cannot fathom what our families endure. Elizabeth Dole's Hidden Hero movement is effective because our spouses are the cornerstone of our rehabilitation. They are our common thread and often the access point to spiritual wellness, because healing happens at home.

Finish Strong

This book would not have come to fruition without my wife. Her patience and courage, her support and encouragement, and her unabated love through my worst moments are why I'm still here. It wasn't the medical community, counselors, or medication that held me on course; it was my Hidden Hero. I would be but a flag on the shelf if it weren't for her, a fading memory, a statistic. Fulfilling the work God trained me for is happening because of my helpmate. My life is nothing more than forty-plus years of training for this moment in time to deliver this book to you. Our crossroads intersect here and now. That hero complex you carry around keeps you imprisoned. Fighting alone will end in defeat.

Call in reinforcements and accept that the only way forward is through the Cross. You're a significant sheepdog who's trodden in trauma. Rise, warrior, and allow your fall to be your moment of glory. Get back on your feet, stay positive, and finish strong. That which you face has already been conquered. It isn't the perils of time, the torment of sleeplessness, or the volatility of ambition. It's the purpose in which we were created, our discovery of meaning in life, and our reason to carry on. Don't quit on us because you are irreplaceable. Live—if not for you, for them.

You must survive before you can thrive. I dare you to reroute your consciousness to adorn love, mercy, and grace. Allow death to happen on God's time and stop trying to control everything. Prepare for your moment, live for faith and family, and die without regret. Focus on your ten life elements and that which you can control. Let everything else flow by like a mountain stream on a summer morning while fly-fishing for trout. Just think of how tasty those rainbow's will be after cooking them over an open fire.

10

THE CHRISTIAN
ADVENTURE NETWORK

The Christian Adventure Network, known as 10 CAN, Inc., was created to be an innovative ministry for military and first responder families. It connects Christian outdoorsmen with warriors, women, and youth across the world to go hunting, fishing, exploring, and adventuring. We unite and empower believers to use their God-given talents and passion, as they're able, to help those who sacrificed dearly for our freedom. It synergizes communities, volunteers, and organizations to unite on the front line against suicide and internal tyranny.

Free from religious and political aspirations, the primary objective is to lead our heroes to God for moral healing, raise up the next generation of warriors equipped for battle, and restore hope through family adventures. Healing hidden wounds requires an individualized holistic approach. Adolescent development is the key to a resilient future warrior. Searching for world peace? Consider becoming a member of this Kingdom-driven mission.

Synergy is often spoken of in businesses and other organizations, but few know how to function synergistically. The US military provides a perfect illustration—harnessing collaboration to achieve large-scale mission success. Law enforcement and fire-rescue groups have made progress in working together since 9/11. Enterprises support charitable causes, while volunteers rally to help communities. But what about not-for-profits and religious organizations?

These two services for hope are not well known for their synergy. Instead, they are competitive. This nonsense has no place in charitable endeavors. Constrained by our philosophical biases, we restrict ourselves through control mechanisms that originate from fear of loss. We do not want to jeopardize the mission, give up control, or serve in vain. We want our time - our lives to mean something.

According to *Webster's Dictionary*, *synergy* is the effect of combining action or operations to gain mutually beneficial results. If we take that definition literally, then wouldn't the Church be the perfect place for synergy? The Church is, in my own words, a group of people who have a common interest and hold the same belief in a higher power. We believe in doing God's work here on earth. We assemble in church to grow and become better citizens based on lessons taught by people who are called by God and appointed by humans. It comprises individualistic aspirations united for the Kingdom. God creates every person with unique identifiers. Church attendees assimilate for shared goals, but what happens when leaders refuse to collaborate?

The Christian Adventure Network rescues souls through innovative collaboration. Individualism is important, especially when you stand in front of God. However, common denominators unify our efforts to heal spiritual infections. The thread among warriors must be God, family, and country. Any deviation results in isolation, anger, resentment, and hopelessness. By demonstrating God's love through action, adventure, and the great outdoors, we achieve mission success. Connecting warriors with resources that specialize in certain areas, including churches, activates synergy.

Restoring family is a vital part of the rehabilitation process. Harnessing talents can build community impact agents. Returning to childhood roots fosters joy by focusing on the five senses that resurrects positive memories. For this reason, it's important that we invest in a warrior's legacy—their children.

One goal is to create a smooth reintegration platform for veterans into their communities, churches, and families. Educating public leaders, employers, church staff, and citizens eases the burden of a warriors' transition. Coaching warriors on trigger safeguards and community involvement rekindles purpose. The rehabilitation model we use is a revival of mind, body, and soul through adventures that stimulate a "Warrior Up" attitude. Functioning as an impact agent for God, we strive to be the connective tissue between the Church and warriors.

Church autonomy is good, but I believe it can also be like the walls of Jericho. We must march around these walls until they fall, to gain access to the spiritual well that relieves our unquenchable thirst. Don't misunderstand me. I'm not talking about destroying churches or sowing dissension, but rather destroying the pride and arrogance that separate God from humans: the "holier than though" attitude that separates Christians. It's about revitalizing functionality beyond the walls, restoring church unity, and taking back our communities from political correctness, legalities, and hypersensitivity. We must see the value in one another. Abstain from rude or disrespectful behavior: such as ignoring, overlooking, being snobby, spreading rumors, cutting in line, interrupting, making empty promises, shunning, political maneuvering, being conniving, being in closed-door cliques, or even being inaccessible.

The demographics of veterans and first responders are individuals from all walks of life, in every community around America. Churches must be receptive and accessible to sheepdogs. It's been my experience that most churches only seek sheep. Many warriors do not fit the mold for this, so they seek God elsewhere. That's where the Christian Adventure Network comes into play.

Unifying the Church in the face of denominational segregation is only possible through God. As heavenly operators, we serve as a common denominator to bridge this gap. We give warriors a purpose in the Church, through a church, for the Church. We demonstrate how exciting life can be after salvation. Many believe that redemption equals a monotone and boring life, coloring inside the lines, and living within a religious box. That's not the case with us – we're adventurous social impact agents free from the spirit of condemnation. We thrive in fellowship with God through one another. Nature nurtures and is a source of life. We draw fire from the enemy, sharpen one another, and fight side by side. Our goals are to revive heroes, raise the next generation of warriors, and restore families.

The prescription for joy, peace, and happiness encompasses a whole-team concept. Your cure for PTS is the synergistic effect among ten life elements that balances life's priorities for holistic wellness. It's an antiseptic for spiritual infections that can heal moral wounds—a compound with multiple ingredients designed to renew life.

Warriors seek unity, the fellowship of like-minded brothers and sisters who "get it," and freedom from hypocritical judgment. We are real people in unoppressive environments. Control mechanisms, like working security, provide comfort. However, when I coach warriors in church attendance, I always advise them to sit up front. Giving up control is the first step to receiving peace. Sitting in the back of a church provokes hypervigilance and breeds traumatic thoughts. *What if a gunman comes through this door, a bomb is in that bag, or someone rushes the preacher?* Your thoughts begin to control you, and you miss the message, ultimately forgoing the spiritual nourishment you so desperately need. Trust your training and your ability to react (a time-sensitive response for warriors) accordingly.

Incorporating programs that enable dynamic collaboration fosters healthier communities, impact-driven warriors, a better America, and ultimately world peace. When disasters strike, we typically set aside our differences and work together. Outside threats create group integration. We should stimulate this compassion for one another daily. Everyone's story is as unique as your thumbprint. Childhood experiences can predetermine your interpretation of a traumatic event. Sometimes it stimulates a drive to help others who suffer what you have endured; it may lure you into a dark area that instigates a cycle of self-destructive behavior; or it may sharpen your iron, harden your vessel, and create resilience.

Dr. Rhawn Joseph wrote, "Within the core of each of us is the child we once were. This child constitutes the foundation of what we have become, who we are, and what we will be." We have the free will to choose our paths and to decide how we act. We carry burdens on our shoulders that allow us to exercise spiritual fortitude. The more we use it, the stronger we become.

We never receive more than we can handle, although those at their wit's end may disagree. Many are haunted by the things they have seen, smelled, heard, or touched. It is not uncommon to feel out of control. You can either accept the victimology of your tragedy and let it define the remainder of your life, or you can deny its hold on you and move forward. The sense of entitlement that plagues our culture has infiltrated our warrior community. Warriors who feel entitled have lost their warrior ethos. We earned our stripes and now must earn our day. The burden of life is on your shoulders; it is your responsibility—own it.

You can submit to temptations and make poor decisions, or you can focus on productiveness. In either case, you'll note that mastering yourself is a lifelong journey. Come as you are, offer what you can, and let's grow together.

Individualism within the Church detracts from organizational effectiveness. Churches that operate outside of the synergistic circle reduce the efficiency of their ministry. The Church is the body of Christ, a group of people who believe and worship God Almighty. Separation and segregation were around at the beginning. Even Jesus's disciples had disagreements (Acts 15:39). I think, however, that we can overcome this division and unite as one if we "come to Jesus as a child" (Matthew 18:3). You see, children do not ponder on theology or individualism; they seek to fit in and live a simplistic lifestyle. They are often more receptive than adults because they still believe anything's possible.

The only way for the Church to unite, however, is for church leaders to submit their authority and governance to one another, to relinquish a self-perpetuating desire for growth and prosperity, to respect others we disagree with, and to join forces as equals in the sight of God. I do not believe this to be possible without a church revolution, though. We've grown complacent with specific styles of worship, preaching, community service, and the like. We create circles within the Church to protect ourselves and maintain motivation, but the way we do it shows us unreceptive to outsiders, unlike Jesus. We discern who accesses our flock to ensure the sheep do not stray—which is good, but we often miss divine messengers. We focus our efforts on geographic desires and commune with those who share common ground. We are both beneficial and detrimental to the Kingdom. So how do we unite? How do we overcome our human nature?

Uniting the Church

A time is coming when all believers will assemble as one. That time doesn't have to wait for Jesus's return; it can happen now. At this very moment, as you're reading this book, you may be able to think of a couple of churches you'd like to see unite. For one reason or another, you either reached out and they never responded, or someone like me reached out to you and you allowed skepticism to grasp your spirit. Humility and acceptance are the only way for us to collaborate and create synergy for the Kingdom.

For us to let the wedge of misunderstanding interfere with our mutual purpose demonstrates immaturity in spirit. For us to remain skeptical without inquiry proves our complacency in spirit. For us to allow indifference to govern our relationships is to illustrate rebellion in spirit. For us to permit a drawback to hinder progress is to have doubt in spirit. Are you ready to risk it all and overcome yourself as a hindrance to God's plan?

As an educator and trainer, I teach decision-making skills, among many other lessons. The most significant real-time decisions are made after conducting a quick evaluation of risk versus reward. It may appear daunting at first, but once you get the hang of it, it becomes you. Weighing risk versus reward can very well help you resolve many life problems. A good rule of thumb is to never make decisions under emotional duress. Anger, passion, hunger, hurt, and anxiety can lead to rash decisions.

Zig Ziglar says that it is good to respond and bad to react, as with taking medication. If your body responds to a drug, it is good. If you have a reaction, it is bad. So, you have a decision to make: either progress as a unified force against evil or remain segregated by theology. For the sake of the Church and our freedom of religion, I urge you to accept this invitation to unify. It isn't me but the Holy Spirit who is knocking at your door.

The Church is not immune to academic persuasion. For years I was taught to believe that only leaders are successful, pushed to attend college, and influenced by industrialized education. This masterful plan unhinged our workforce and planted a seed of incohesive behavior. We lack trust for one another, fail to comply, and live rebelliously. We're top-heavy on leaders and lack qualified followers. Most people would choose to recreate the wheel rather than join forces. We're unique—that's agreeable—but the common good is not. Righteousness is not open to interpretation. The gray area is a trap, a bridge that leads to darkness. Many churches stand in the light and call to those in darkness but refuse to cross the bridge. On the other hand, the Christian Adventure Network does not let public opinion influence the mission. In no form or fashion does this insinuate that we're superior to churches. It merely means that we can cross thresholds that churches won't, goes places that churches don't, and rescue wounded heroes from the darkness. We are a proponent of the Church, a tactical element focused on warriors, a complementary service to increase the kingdom with military and first-responder families. We are a force multiplier, a catalyst for growth. But we need a lighthouse for our return, a place to recharge, a church home.

Church leaders, this is an opportunity to go places you've never been before. Jesus was a friend to sinners. He went where Pharisees wouldn't and condemned them for having more interest in public relations than winning souls. If you have a desire to leave the ninety-nine sheep to rescue the one but fear public opinion, then reach out. We can operate discreetly or draw fire for you. In either case, we're here to complement your divine calling.

The Sheepdog

Growing up in church, I learned a little about the behavior of sheep and shepherds. The term *sheepdog* didn't exist that I knew of. I learned this word when I became a shepherd of my own flock of sheep. The daunting task of protecting a herd of sheep from predators and themselves was a twenty-four-hour chore. It's a way of life that allows little time for anything else.

Those who stood at the pulpit and preached to me about being a shepherd had no real experience with four-legged sheep. In a way, sheep and goats are like people: the grass is greener on the other side (discontent), they'll consume food that leads to poor health or death (self-destructive), they combat for position (leadership), and they like to stick together (metropolitan and urban communities). Both sheep and goats are prone to enemy attacks, but goats are more defensive, stubborn, and rebellious. Sheep are gentle and submissive for the most part. You drive goats but lead sheep.

The most significant difference between sheep and goats, in my opinion, is that sheep all think alike, whereas each goat has a mind of its own. Sheep rarely fight back but will stand their ground when necessary. They have little experience with self-defense, so when combating a predator, they usually perish. Therefore, a sheepdog is vital to the flock.

The shepherd can live peacefully when the sheepdog is at work. Shepherds use intellect, but sheepdogs are battle-hardened warriors. They will fight to the death to serve their purpose. Shepherds adore these protectors, but they're uneasy around them as well. The fear that, one day, sheepdogs may turn violent hinders relationships between the flock and the sheepdog, creating dissension and loneliness. This four-legged warrior serves and protects until its last breath. The sheep know the sheepdog but abstain from befriending him. They commune under the sheepdog's protection.

Sheep follow the shepherd in droves. They are content in the herd and find refuge together. They don't fight when under attack but rely on the shepherd or sheepdog to defend them. Their most significant contribution is multiplying and growing the herd.

Shepherds cannot increase their flocks. Their purpose is to lead the sheep to water and green pastures, maintain assembly, and protect them from both inside and outside danger. If left unchecked, worms or disease can destroy flocks from the inside. Complacent or distracted shepherds will miss this and lose many. Often, distractions come from outside threats, which is why sheepdogs are so valuable. Good shepherds will interact and trust their herds' protectors, understanding that sheepdogs require special attention. This relationship is unequivocally mutual, and input from sheepdogs should garner a response. But what happens when other sheepdogs show up?

The initial reaction when a new sheepdog shows up is often distrust. By nature, sheepdogs are combative, and shepherds know this. Their approach at first may be aggressive to scare off the new sheepdog, but they often shift to compassion. The new dog's initial reaction is also distrust, and it stays on the edge in case it needs to make a quick escape from a stone-throwing shepherd. This ploy is temporary, though. Establishing trust makes them members of the defense team, not the flock. Just don't wait so long to determine trustworthiness; if you do, the sheepdog may venture back into the wilderness.

Sheepdogs rally: they don't flock. This is akin to military and first-responder warriors. They save lives, stand between good and evil, defend their teams, and go to war when necessary. When sheepdogs retire, they don't become sheep; they remain warriors. Their experiences afford them a unique relationship with the shepherd. When a warrior and a preacher better understand the nature of each other's positions, they begin to function synergistically. The warrior becomes part of the team, and the preacher can focus on internal threats. Hope prospers when this mutually beneficial relationship occurs.

Key to Hope

There is never an absence of hope, but rather a lack of faith. As an adventurous teenager, I often found myself in dangerous circumstances. One day, while exploring a cave, I was overtaken by fear. Crawling through a small entryway with just a flashlight, head tilted sideways and arms flat to my side, I squeezed through nearly twenty yards of tunnel to reach an open cavern. I was in the Appalachian Mountains exploring a cave with my father. We were working on restoring a broken relationship that resulted from his abandoning us as children. As we navigated through the dark earthy crevasses, I noticed several new rockfalls. In less than an hour, we had reached the end of the cave at nearly five hundred yards deep. We turned off our lights and sat silently. The loud sound of nothingness permeated my eardrums. The absence of light hindered any possibility of sight. I felt blind and deaf, and my immediate perspective was, *what a hopeless situation this would be*. Without artificial light, we would spend days trying to resurface. Luckily, we were prepared and began our ascent.

As we neared the entrance, I observed the glimmer of light shimmering into the cave. I felt an overwhelming sense of joy, but fear grasped my soul. A feeling of claustrophobia began to transcend my confidence. *What if the narrow tunnel inhibits my exit? I barely fit coming in. Will the earth let me escape her clutches?* A severe feeling of doom loomed over me as I neared the squeeze shoot. I resisted the urge to panic but hesitated for a moment to gather myself. Sanity verged on insanity, but in a moment of hopelessness, my father stepped up. A bigger man than me at the time, he said, "Son, follow me." He led me across the bridge from darkness to the light. It was a terrifying experience that strengthened my resolve. It was more difficult to cross back into the light than to stay in the dark. The insurmountable fear of failure to recover and of imprisonment took courage to overcome. I knew the way out was forward, but I needed support.

Often, we find hope in unsuspecting places. Sometimes it's a symbol like the US flag, a leader like Andrew Young Jr., or a broken parent like my father. Recognizing your key to hope is of utmost importance.

The Roman Empire ruthlessly ruled over millions of people, enslaving, torturing, taxing, imprisoning, and dictating as they pleased. There's no telling how many died by suicide or how many endured the suffering awaiting change. Those who took their own lives lost one thing that those who survived held onto—hope. Hope is the essence of desire. Leaders know it as an energetic force that drives change. Evil rulers seek to dictate hope, whereas righteous monarchs arouse it. For centuries, people have found faith in symbols. Though one of the Ten Commandments is not to make any graven image to worship, we've idolized the Cross as the symbol of Christianity and hope. It reminds us of the sacrifice, the blood of the Lamb, and the resurrecting power of God. The Cross has been used by good and evil alike because it is one of the most powerful symbols ever to exist. But it's not welcomed by those who fear, misunderstand, are skeptical, or are indifferent to it.

Christ followers were hunted after the crucifixion of Jesus. Some felt driven to retaliate and defend their homes, while others became martyrs or evaded capture. Those who escaped persecution used a pagan symbol—a fish—to communicate with one another in secret. This symbol was used as a code for Christians to network. It became the very icon that allowed disciples to press forward in spreading the gospel.

When Christians approached an unfamiliar face, they would draw half of the fish in the sand. If the other person completed the fish design, they knew they were in good company. The fish symbolized hope in times of sorrow and dread. It enabled code talk for operators. It reminds us of several great miracles performed by Jesus and that is important in times of doubt. For these reasons, it is the core icon that establishes the 10 CAN logo. It is the bridge between church and state, politics and religion, science and spirituality.

Look closely at our logo and see if you can decipher all the codes. Do you see the fish, or do you see a ribbon? Ribbons incite hope as well, but not in the spiritual sense. Now that you understand the central element of our logo and purpose, allow me to decode the rest. The fish doubles as an adult lifting a child to the stars. The stars represent the five branches of the armed forces. The thin blue line represents law enforcement, and the thin red line represents fire-rescue. It has a black background, symbolizing our work in dark places. The two circles represent our eternal life and the defense of the inner circle. The three words at the bottom, *Honor, Revive, Grow*, name our three purposes. The top is in Latin (*Et Familia Fidem*) because the US Government wouldn't allow us to display our banner on their properties in the English translation (Faith and Family). Our logo is coded to cross cultural boundaries and to build relationships with warriors.

Bridging the gap between the light and the darkness requires us to operate in between. Perception is reality to most people. Churches fear accusations of devious or lewd behavior, and for good reason. Opinions are often misinformed. Many believe themselves to be subject matter experts, devolving with each keystroke in hurtful and uneducated input. We've become such a hypersensitive culture that everything is offensive. Political correctness governs our freedom of speech, and public opinion sways the line between right and wrong.

Now you see why churches have boundaries. In the sense of geographic reach, Jesus had no limitations, no thresholds, no restrictions. He commanded that we go to all nations of the world (Matthew 28:19). He was a friend to sinners and drew them from their ways. Spiritually speaking, 10 CAN runs tactical missions into the darkness to rescue POWs. If you've ever had the privilege of meeting or hearing testimonies from POWs, you'll note that hope helped them persevere in perilous times. They were held against their will, threatened with death, and tortured. Their faith fueled their hope, allowing them to survive that grave situation.

No matter where you are, what you endure, why you're there, or when you'll dig out, you must pivot to escape spiritual captivity. You discover your pivot point when you see the light through the darkness. It is a path and a bridge to escape the self-destructive nature of PTS and other psychological matters. It is a map to joy, peace, and prosperity. It'll navigate you through dense forest, open plains, thick swamps, and mountaintops. A wilderness experience will exploit your vulnerabilities, strengthen your resilience, and realign your perspective. The natural remedy for hope is nature. Are you ready to find freedom outdoors, or will you wallow in self-pity and remain a spiritual POW?

Do It Outdoors

Growing up in poverty, I learned to hunt and fish for sustenance. My father taught me survival skills before he left, and afterward, my mom remained steadfast in raising us on the farm. Though my siblings and I put her through it, she persevered and kept the faith that her efforts would not be in vain (Proverbs 22:6). My roots grew deep in the outdoors while hunting frogs, squirrels, rabbits, raccoons, and birds of all sorts as well as fishing, growing, and gathering food. I was the Daniel Boone of Blueberry Hill, a name my cousin and I gave to our thirty-acre farm. Those childhood roots prepared me for the impact of war. They kept me grounded and fortified through the storm.

In my experience, rural, urban, and metropolitan areas all serve a purpose in wellness, but that purpose is sometimes counterintuitive. Often, urban and metropolitan areas are detrimental to mental health, while rural areas, parks, and nature are instrumental. In the former, however, beneficial services like yoga, cognitive talk therapy, counseling, support groups, exposure therapy, art, music, entertainment, medicine, and more are offered. In the latter, opportunities like horseback riding, farming, hunting, fishing, spending time in nature, and walk abouts are available. Figuring out how to balance each resource to complement your foundation can be a struggle.

Having roots in the outdoors proves most effective. It may be different for you, but nature should remain an element of your healing. I'd rather abstain from society, but human contact is a vital proponent of healing. We are catalysts of God's blessings for one another. After all, people are His greatest creation.

A well-balanced lifestyle will produce whole health. Both rural and urban areas are home to people with diverse cultural backgrounds. Some people are content with metal forests and paved parks, while others seek life-giving trees, dirt, and predictable animals. It is not good to remain in one element too long, though. Jesus found sanctuary in the wilderness, but He was also tempted there (Matthew 4:1–11). He maintained a delicate balance between the two arenas, navigating the threshold between God's greatest creation and His prescription for us (nature). When balancing your time, consider weighing your duty against desire.

Religion vs. Relationship

In a world driven by competition and challenges to be the best, we discover that many of our decisions are made sentimentally. Religion versus relationship, for example, compares duty and desire. For many, it's a choice of one or the other. The duty to fulfill your military obligation overrules your desire for home. Being religious requires the same type of emotional discipline as being a warrior. You're bound by your oath to fulfill mission assignments, team requirements, training, and so on. If you've never served in the military, law enforcement, or fire-rescue, then you'll not grasp how much sacrifice occurs. We follow strict guidelines, execute protocols, and carry out our assignments without consideration for our own lives.

Martyrs, like Dr. Martin Luther King Jr., understood that there is no gain without sacrifice and that each life is but a grain of sand on a beach comprised of innumerable other grains of sand. He, like the American soldier, firefighter, law enforcement officer, and paramedic, bought in to the ideology of duty. They were not driven solely by desire but by duty to their fellow humans.

Those with less discipline typically leave a smaller footprint. The manifestation of their desires comes to fruition through their behavior. Character reveals itself between duty and desire. Commitment alone cannot drive people to sacrifice themselves for others. It is an emotional context that directs our decision-making skills in the heat of the moment. Moral order and relational commitment go hand in hand. However, relational emotions tend to be influenced by contemporary thought, current ideologies, and social norms. When suicide was alleged to be the ultimate sin that punched your ticket to hell, the rates were much lower (Hedegaard, Curtin, & Warner, 2018). When loyalty to your spouse and parental pride were popular, divorce rates were lower (Hempstead & Phillips, 2015). When policymakers and public leaders allow emotion to triumph over duty, we find an unbalance that breeds chaos and undisciplined citizens.

Government entities have become strong in rules and regulations but weak in character. You do not have to choose between religion and relationship as they go together. Duty cannot be exemplified without desire. A competitive nature doesn't always have to result in defiance. Challenging yourself to be the best you is a personal duty to enhance emotional character. Eliminating options can help reduce stress and increase peace. You can be religious and relational. You should be!

Studying the Bible is comparable to engaging in military continuation training. Religion, like a service commitment, requires you to gain readiness. While serving requires you to be cognitively and physically fit to fight, religion fortifies your spirituality. Some religions do not accept the relationship between theologians and anti-theologians. Both parties extract biblical aspects that satisfy their emotional desires and justify cultural biases. In my opinion, they are 50 percent right and 50 percent wrong. The Bible is old and new, not old *or* new.

In comparison (Old Testament vs. New Testament), you may find an angry God versus a loving God, condemnation versus salvation, and rules versus relationships. Some choose to satisfy emotional desires by focusing on one or the other, but it is vital to maintain the assembly of the two. Duty cannot abound without passion, and desire alone detracts from our effectiveness.

Everyone is on an individual journey. Journeys require us to travel using maps. A good one will help you predict the road that lies ahead, guide you along safe paths, and keep you pointed in the right direction. The Bible is this map for your life's journey. Without it, you're navigating based on roads you've already traveled. Your experiences and rearing can be your moral compass, but what happens when that compass is compromised?

Anyone with tactical training understands the importance of using proven maps. Don't go into a hostile situation with untested material. We live in a dangerous world, be it danger to ourselves or toward each other. We must open the map and get back on course. Don't be that prideful person who keeps driving. Stop and ask for directions. Be both dutiful and relational.

What's in the CAN?

Inside the CAN is a vast network of formidable men, women, and children devoted to saving souls. Bridging the gap between the warrior and the Church is part of the vision, as is uniting the Church from denominational segregation. The Christian Adventure Network is a segue for these concepts to become a reality. Our mission is to light up the darkness. By shining light on the path instead of in your face, we believe we can help you in traveling toward holistic wellness. Preventing suicides, healing traumatic stress, taking proactive steps for mental health, and bringing peace that passes all understanding are part of a cure for the spiritual infection that has our heroes fighting for their lives.

10 CAN produces synergy for the countless independent endeavors hoping to make a positive impact on our warriors. It is the glue that pulls the charity puzzle together - uniting the Church, nonprofits, and volunteers. It is the glimmer of light in a dark cave. It is a symbol of hope for the hopeless, a road map for the lost, and a tactical rescue team for spiritual POWs. Balancing between cities and forests aids in the effort to find purpose and have peace. There are pros and cons to both, and too much of either can prove detrimental.

Sheep often misunderstand sheepdogs, but a well-trained shepherd will find value in these warriors. They have a purpose beyond their prime and can offer exceptional defense against outside attacks. Ultimately, we're all on a journey, whether we're sheep or sheepdogs. Shepherds guide, but they often prevent us from unifying with the ultimate flock. It is our destiny to be both duty-bound and relationship driven. See the Bible as a road map for your journey, not a governing authority hindering your fun. Join the Christian Adventure Network and breach the denominational walls of Jericho.

Hoorah Therapy

Want to know what makes us different? It's our simple approach to life—getting back to basics. It is the acceptance of our fate, the denial of fear, and boldness to hold the line. We acknowledge the benefits of "soft therapies" but realize that some warriors need a more aggressive approach. Yoga and counseling work for some, but others need to kick in doors, jump out of airplanes, or wrestle alligators.

I designed Hoorah therapy to meet the demand for warriors who were not benefiting from common practices. It stimulates healing, purpose, and meaning for men and women who live adventurously. These warriors are mission oriented and purpose-driven, and they love the great outdoors. Hoorah therapy isn't for everyone, though. It's for those who want to live full speed.

Warriors know what it means to have skin in the game. For me, I want every single day to matter. Making a positive difference in my family, community, and church drives my adventurous spirit. If you refuse handouts but desire a hand up to earn it, then you're in the right spot. Warriors are eager to do life abundantly, without excuse or blame, in service to God and community.

Hoorah therapy is an unconventional approach to health and wellness. Sessions include but are not limited to hunting, fishing, survival, scuba diving, spelunking, back country exploration, rock climbing, whitewater rafting, ski-diving, and more. If you dreamed it as a child, let us help you pursue it as a warrior. You can put your health and wellness in someone else's hands, or you can grab the reins and ride off into the sunset.

Bravery is defying your fears and mustering the intestinal fortitude to courageously move forward into oncoming fire, especially when failure is imminent. Typically, warriors do not self-proclaim their heroic nature. Not everyone in the military is a warrior, and not all warriors have heroic tendencies. However, anyone can be a hero at any given time. F. Scott Fitzgerald wrote, "Show me a hero, and I'll write you a tragedy." But I leave you with this, that if anything's impossible, try anyways. You have nothing to lose and everything to gain. This is your life. Live it adventurously!

BIBLIOGRAPHY

American Indian Legends. "Two Wolves: A Cherokee Legend." *First People.* n.d. Retrieved from https://www.firstpeople.us/FP-Html-Legends/TwoWolves-Cherokee.html.

Barton, J., and M. Rogerson. "The Importance of Greenspace for Mental Health." *BJPsych Int.* 14, no. 4 (Nov. 2017): 79–81. Retrieved from https://www.ncbi.nlm.nih.gov/pmc/articles/PMC5663018/

Bibleinfo. "Sabbath." Retrieved on September 16, 2019, from http://www.bibleinfo.com/en/topics/sabbath

Bloomer, R. J., M. M. Kabir, R. E. Canale, J. F. Trepanowski, K. E. Marshall, T. M. Farney, and K. G. Hammond. "Effect of a 21-Day Daniel Fast on Metabolic and Cardiovascular Disease Risk Factors in Men and Women." National Library of Medicine, National Institute of Health. Retrieved from https://www.ncbi.nlm.nih.gov/pmc/articles/PMC2941756/

Brainy Quotes. BrainyMedia, Inc. 2019. Retrieved from www.brainyquote.com

De Moor, M. H. M., A. L. Beem, J. H. Stubbe, D. I. Boomsma, and E. J. C. De Geus. "Regular Exercise, Anxiety, Depression, and Personality: A Population-Based Study." Preventive Medicine 42, no. 4 (April 2006): 273–279. Retrieved from https://doi.org/10.1016/j.ypmed.2005.12.002

Folkins, C. H., and W. E. Sime. "Physical Fitness Training and Mental Health."

American Psychologist 36, no. 4 (1981): 373–389. Retrieved from http://dx.doi.org/10.1037/0003-066X.36.4.373.

Hedegaard, H., S. C. Curtin, and M. Warner. "Suicide Rates in the United States Continue to Increase." NCHS Data Brief, no 309. Hyattsville, MD: National Center for Health Statistics.

Hempstead, K. A., and J. A. Phillips. "Rising Suicide among Adults Aged 40–64 Years: The Role of Job and Financial Circumstances." *American Journal of Preventive Medicine* 48, no. 5 (2015): 491–500.

Hu, G., H. C. Wilcox, L. Wissow, and S. P. Baker. "Mid-life Suicide: An Increasing Problem in U.S. Whites, 1999–2005." *American Journal of Preventive Medicine* 37, no. 6 (2009):579.

Katz, B. "Does Exposure to Green Spaces in Childhood Lead to Better Mental Health?" *Smithsonian Institute.* February 2019. Retrieved from https://www.smithsonianmag.com/smart-news/does-exposure-green-spaces-childhood-lead-better-mental-health-180971590/

Lanza, I. R., D. K. Short, K. R. Short, S. Raghavakaimal, R. Basu, M. J. Joyner,

J. P. McConnell, and K. S. Nair. "Endurance Exercise as a Countermeasure for Aging." American Diabetes Association. 2008. Retrieved from https://diabetes.diabetesjournals.org/content/57/11/2933.short

Lee, L., M. Roser, and E. Ortiz-Ospina. "Suicide." *Our World in Data.* 2019. Retrieved from https://ourworldindata.org/suicide

Morabia, A., and M. C. Costanza. "Does Walking 15 Minutes per Day Keep the Obesity Epidemic Away? Simulation of the Efficacy of a Population-Wide Campaign." *American Journal of Public Health* 94, no. 3 (March 1, 2004): 437–440. Retrieved from https://ajph.aphapublications.org/doi/full/10.2105/AJPH.94.3.437

Rampell, C. "Money Fights Predict Divorce Rates." *New York Times,* Economics

Blog. 2009. Retrieved from http://www.usu.edu/today/pdf/2009/december/itn120709377.pdf

Ruiz, R. "One Overlooked Way We Can Significantly Improve Our Mental Health: More Nature." *Mashable.* 2019. Retrieved from https://mashable.com/video/apple-dark-mode-ios/

Sandoiu, A. "What Religion Does to Your Brain." *Medical News Today.* 2018. Retrieved from https://www.medicalnewstoday.com/articles/322539.php

Ullah, H., M. Akhtar, and F. Hussain. "Effects of Sugar, Salt, and Distilled Water on White Blood Cells and Platelet Cells." *Journal of Tumor* 4, no. 1 (2015): 354–358. Retrieved from http://www.ghrnet.org/index.php/jt/article/view/1340

Warren, Rick. *Purpose-Driven Life.* City: Publisher, 2002.

Weir, K. "Worrying Trends in U.S. Suicide Rates." *American Psychological Association* 50, no. 3 (2019). Retrieved from https://www.apa.org/monitor/2019/03/trends-suicide

Wood, L., P. Hooper, S. Foster, and F. Bull. "Public Green Spaces and Positive

Mental Health: Investigating the Relationship between Access, Quantity and Types of Parks and Mental Well-being." *Health & Place* 48 (Nov 2017): 63–71.